Sheltering Tree

"Friendship Is a Sheltering Tree . . . ."

Youth and Age
Samuel Taylor Coleridge

Mrs. Louis A. Sohier, Concord

ON MAY MORNINGS

Sheltering Tree

A Story of the Friendship of

RALPH WALDO EMERSON
and
AMOS BRONSON ALCOTT

BY

HUBERT H. HOELTJE

KENNIKAT PRESS, INC./PORT WASHINGTON, N. Y.

SHELTERING TREE

TO THE MEMORY OF MY WIFE

PAULINE MARIE BUSHNELL HOELTJE

FOREWORD

THIS IS THE STORY of two lives, of a friendship, and of a way of interpreting the world. Emerson, of course, was the greater man. He remains "the outstanding figure of American letters" (Paul Elmer More); his volumes are still "the mirror of the American soul" (James Truslow Adams); and in him we find "the one citizen of the New World fit to have his name uttered in the same breath with that of Plato" (John Dewey). If Alcott was the lesser man, he was nevertheless Emerson's most intimate friend, known and loved for almost fifty years, the one companion in whose presence Emerson most clearly became aware of his own thoughts. In different ways, both found strength in their friendship.

This is not a critical biography. If any criticism appears, it is (for the author) an inescapable friction of the machinery of composition. The attempt rather is to permit the characters to speak their own thoughts, as colored by their own feelings. The point of view is internal and emotional rather than external and intellectually aloof.

The method employed is very simple. Whenever possible, and this is for the most part, the very language of the characters is employed—their voluminous diaries (as well as other primary sources) providing ample material from which to draw. The function of the author has been merely to select and to join, and this function he has tried to perform sympathetically and without violating the tenor of the whole.

Here are two of the most interesting literary men America has yet produced, and here is the story of the most fruitful literary relationship in our annals. The thoughts of these men—their feelings, their times—are, it is hoped, embodied in this story of their friendship.

H. H. H.

Iowa City, Iowa.

CONTENTS

Sheltering Tree

THIS THROBBING HEART

FOR SEVERAL WEEKS the woods had been all in a glow. Every tree had put on an autumnal tint. The white ash, which the other day had been of a mulberry hue, now vied with the black oak in its redness. The old leaves of the pitch pine reflected a golden yellow, only less bright than the yellow that shimmered from the maples. What a rare light was that which hovered over the Old Manse as the sun struck the yellow willows! It was a world of reds and yellows, though the river was never more sky-blue than on these clear afternoons—blue, and white as milk where some freak of light struck it aslant. The nights had been cool now, and it required only the gentlest puff of wind to bring down a shower of elm leaves. In the woods the ground was covered with fallen leaves—oak and maple and chestnut—which crackled briskly underfoot, their aroma suggesting fresh linen and hours of deep, healthful sleep. Along the stone walls, on the hills, the frost had stripped the vines of the grape, and there, on the ground, lay the fruit, plump and bursting with ripeness, and fragrant of long summer days. In the orchards, under the trees, had been piled heaps of apples. There was about them a cidery odor that vaguely prophesied winter evenings and friendly conversation.

These matters seemed simple enough; but the haze of these afternoons, the tantalizing scents which rose at evening, the moonlit fogs which hung over the river at night— who could read their meaning? What was it that Nature wished to say?

II

In the midst of a riotous profusion of color, lay a tree-covered range of hills, their placid slopes overlooking the meadows of Mill Brook, where once the red men trod. Here, beneath these hills, the white settlers made their dug-out huts, and here, from Revolutionary times, had stood these mellowing houses. It was a tedious and homely old road that ran at the foot of these hills—the Great Road from Boston—tedious and dusty with the traffic of an endless procession of wagons carrying the commerce to the farthest villages of New Hampshire and Vermont. Along this road, too, came the daily coaches from Boston, a three-hour ride when the weather was fair, as it was now. Today, when Bronson Alcott stepped to the ground after such a ride, it was a relief to stretch his legs again. How could he tell, on his first experience with this thoroughfare, that it was bringing him to scenes of which he was to be for-ever a part, to a man, only slightly known now, whose constancy through many years was to make him his best benefactor and friend? Today Alcott might cast a casual glance at the old house opposite the lane through the meadow and not give it a second thought. The leaves of the ancient elms by the road might drop today unnoticed into the dust. In days to come, in how many autumns was he not to see them gently fall as he gazed toward the tranquillity of Lincoln Woods and the hidden peace of Walden Water? But how could he foresee that now?

III

When Bronson Alcott came to Concord on that bril-liantly colored day in mid-October, 1835, it was with a mind aflame with enthusiasms. How different now did the world seem than it did scarcely more than a half-dozen years ago when he was a lonely teacher in a district school, eager, but with his mental world all in a turmoil! Was it only in his reading that he found a kinship of thought?[1] So it seemed then, though even books were confusing. Where in them could he find agreement? These philosophers—Locke, and Stewart, and Reid—how hard and sure they seemed! It was a comfort to find life so certain in their hands. But Pascal—he, too, was interesting. "The heart has its reasons, which reason does not know." Was it possible, after all, to refer all ideas to sensation, as Locke said? And then these Swedenborgian sermons—what was to be made of them? Were they fanciful merely, or did they reveal a world of truth more immutable than that of Locke and his school? That little book of the Swedenborgian apothecary—Sampson Reed—how it turned Locke's world upside down! Was it possible, when all was said and done, that the process of learning was not by synthesis or analysis?[2]

Living in Boston had had its merits for Alcott. If the houses of the great and the mighty were not open to an unknown teacher from the country, there were, at any rate, the churches. He was always welcome there. He could hear the best that Boston had to offer, and it always seemed, somehow, more near and real when he heard the spoken word. The book perused in study, however exciting, was impersonal. To be near the thinker was reassuring. Might he not be forgiven a momentary flush of pride, when he recognized as his own the ideas uttered by the great Dr. Channing?[3] These elegant sermons—were they not an expression of Alcott's own criticisms of the popular orthodox dogmas of the day? And in his diary, at least, he might record that the great Boston divine did not go far enough to satisfy his own mind. Alcott might, to be sure, acknowledge the superior excellence of Christianity to all systems of morals, but need he accept the claims which its friends generally attached to it as the ground of its support? Would it not be a higher ground to say that Christianity carried within itself the evidence of its truth? But Channing was unquestionably a great man—Channing and Dr. Follen, who, like all scholarly Germans, was much in advance of most of his English and American contemporaries. When Follen spoke, Alcott felt sure that there were no bounds to the improvableness of human nature. It seemed clear, as he listened to these men and their kind, that the world was ready for some new development, that the old motives by which it had hitherto been governed were giving way to milder and more beneficent promptings of duty. To take a part in such a movement, that would be something worthy of a man's endeavor!

Should his part, however, be in the province of thought or of action? The question puzzled Alcott. On the whole, the province of thought seemed the more promising. It would be an injustice to his powers if he wandered, for outward reasons, into fields more properly belonging to minds of another order. To make the most of his nature in the circumstances of the age, it was necessary to devote his life to free, comparative, universal thought. So it seemed, though the question kept recurring, and never would stay properly settled.

Most difficult of all had been the perplexing problem, in his speculative thought, of perceiving the connections of the material and the spiritual philosophy. What a desert of reading and thinking had been traversed to find the ever-escaping link! Both had their claims, but neither would resolve itself into the other. There, essentially, lay the root of his interest in Locke, and at the same time, in Pascal. It was impossible, of course, to serve both masters forever.

And then two great thinkers had set Alcott's mind at

rest. Always afterward these were lodestars which pointed the way in the midst of the greatest apparent perplexities.

First, there had been Coleridge.[4] In his poetry, what passages of surpassing beauty and deep wisdom! His prose writings, too, were full of splendid ideas clothed in the most awful and imposing imagery. What man, since Jesus, thought Alcott, had penetrated more deeply into the profound mysteries of the human spirit? He was equally at home in the intellectual and spiritual spheres. In him were combined the philosopher and the poet, each reflecting light and beauty on the other. It was he who unshackled one from the philosophy of the senses, and led one to search for the grounds of experience, not in the impressions of external nature, but in the spontaneous life of the Spirit itself, independent of its passage in time and space. The perusal of *Aids to Reflection, The Friend,* and *Biographia Literaria* had opened a new era in Alcott's philosophical life.

Then, too, there had been Plato.[5] Ever since the reading of Richerard and Magendie's *Physiology,* back in Alcott's district-schoolteaching days, Plato had, of course, been a name, but little more. The *Dialogues* themselves, where in America could they be found? It was like discovering a new world—to come at last upon the "Cratylus," the "Phaedo," the "Timaeus," and the "Parmenides" in the translations of Thomas Taylor, with copious notes leading farther and farther into the fallow fields of Greek thought. It was a discovery too rich to be experienced alone. But with whom could it be shared? Who among Alcott's friends had ever heard of Thomas Taylor and his translations?

Plato had completed the liberation which Coleridge had begun. It was his master hand that had—so Alcott thought —finally swept away the clouds to admit the bright light of truth. Now it had become clear beyond a doubt that one would look in vain for a solution of the heart's problem from the skill of the head. Locke with his sensationalism, Bacon with his inductive method, and Aristotle with his fixed bounds—all these had been satisfied with forms agreeable merely to the understanding, had erred in looking outward for the origin of the human powers, making more of phenomena than they ought. But in Plato, as in Jesus, was to be found the Light of the World, that supersensual light accompanying everyone who enters the world of sense and then endeavors to regain that spirit which he seems to have lost by his incarnation. The difficulty with modern philosophy was that it limited itself to a consideration of the finite and the visible, and was therefore incompetent to investigate primary causes and ultimate laws. The boasted acquisitions of natural science were but fragments, unintelligible parts, broken members of a whole whose outline had not been pictured in the ideal, the scientist therefore lacking the standard by which to resolve these parts into their true place in the great Whole. The virtue of the philosophy of Plato was that it had intercommunion with the invisible and the infinite. In it, spirit was all in all—matter its form and shadow. Nature was the emblem of Being; Man, the Incarnate Spirit; and God, the Absolute Spirit. As in the morning twilight the sun points in the horizon the radiant glories of his own visage upon the clear and serene azure, announcing to the risen world the coming day, even so does the Divinity, in this terrestrial life, shed forth on the dim forms of mind and matter some intimation of his own celestial visage. To believe this was to be a Platonist, an idealist, a transcendentalist. To believe this was to cast aside all skepticisms, to attain serenity, and to abound in hope.

IV

It was with such enthusiasms that Bronson Alcott, aged almost thirty-six, came to Concord for the first time to visit Emerson. He came with slight personal acquaintance of the man whose life was to be linked for almost fifty years with his own, but he came with ample reason to believe that he was to meet a kindred spirit. He had heard the young minister deliver, some seven years earlier, at the Church in Channing Place, Boston, a sermon on the Universality of the Notion of Deity, and had thought it a very respectable effort.[6] In these first years of his residence in Boston, he had classified Emerson, as he had George Ripley and others, as one of the lesser lights whom he associated with the great Dr. Channing. Later, after he had opened his famous Temple School, he had heard Emerson deliver his lectures on Michelangelo and Luther. Of both he spoke in praise. Not many men, he thought, took such noble views of the mission of man, or expressed themselves so beautifully and so profoundly. Presently he had invited Emerson and his brother Charles, and his Aunt Mary, to his home—together, however, with others. There was no great degree of intimacy as yet, and the meeting merely represented one of Alcott's initial efforts, made with considerable difficulty, to enter the circle of those whose ideas, but not whose social background, he shared. But it was not long until, in his diary list of the most interesting representatives of what he called the spiritual philosophy, Emerson stood third—Dr. Channing and Dr. Follen standing at the top.[7] It is clear that Emerson was growing in his esteem, and that it needed only a gesture from the younger man to induce Alcott to make a cast for that friendship and that intellectual companionship which he had craved during the many lonely years of his self-education.

V

And Emerson?

As a boy, he had been taught to prize his ancestry, which, with here and there a strange sport, was a matter to be proud of, a diary-keeping ancestry made up, by and large, of Puritan clergymen, deacons, teachers, merchants— some men of wealth, some who prayed for poverty, a prolific family, a frequently marrying group (Rebecca Emerson was married thrice, she being her third husband's fourth wife), an instance of insanity here, a case of unusual mental vigor there, a witch-persecutor early in the American line, a fiery revolutionist for a grandfather.[8] But it was the youthful Emerson's humor to look coolly even at the best elements of his pedigree. The dead, he had decided, might very well sleep in their moonless night; his business was with the living.

At Harvard—seven Emersons had preceded him at Harvard in five generations—he detested mathematics, read Chaucer and Montaigne on the sly, and graduated with a standing somewhat below the average of his class. His professors had hammered Locke and Stewart into him; his Aunt Mary, who had notions of her own, counseled solitude and the reading of Wordsworth.[9] College had not done much for him. Its best service was to provide a chamber for study, and then to interfere only a little. He did not find his stride until later.

After graduation he taught in his brother William's school for young women. He had never associated with girls. There had been many golden hours with his brothers in Peter's Field beyond the Old Manse, but no girls had shared their chivalric world. Now blushes were ill concealed, and yet glances of admiration could not be restrained. Now and all his life he was a shy and innocent admirer of feminine beauty, which he considered the essence of illusion.

It was a relief, when the last class of the day was ended, to dismiss his tormentors and to fly to the wilderness among the bushy hills of Roxbury.

Then came years of great uncertainty, with vast seas of despondency and a small island of poignant happiness quickly submerged. Intermittently he attended Harvard Divinity School, taught again, struggled with weak eyes, and yielded helplessly to the little mice gnawing at his lungs. At last, to avoid the New England winter, he took ship for the South, whiled away the endless Florida days strolling on the beach, tediously drove green oranges over the sand with a stick, wrote sermons which he feared might never be delivered, and stared long hours over the ocean wondering what might lie beyond mortality. It became manifest to him, as he waited thus for an aching chest to mend, that one has seen but half the universe who has never been shown the house of pain.[10]

The return North, when health again permitted, was to supply pulpits as occasion demanded, to read, to think, and to hope as much as he dared. Cautiously he recorded in his diary that he was a bachelor and had never been in love. It was as much as might be said by a young man of twenty-four not out of danger of consumption and with no prospects. It would scarcely do even to admit to himself the vision of happiness which enveloped his mind when he contemplated Ellen's loveliness. And when, at the expiration of a year, he wrote to tell his brother of his engagement, it was to speak of himself as a presumptuous man, though as happy as it was safe in life to be. She was seventeen, he said, and very beautiful. But it was impossible not to be apprehensive, for she shared, in a more violent form, the affliction which had sent him South. They had been married a year and a half when she died. She was then nineteen.

The uncertain years now became tempestuous ones, though the violence of the storm was almost wholly internal, so that only an occasional gust blew into the world of men and action. He had permitted himself to marry because he had been invited to become associate pastor of Old North Church on Hanover Street. It was a church distinguished by the great name of Mather—Increase, Cotton, and Samuel —one of the greatest names in the New England clergy. It was a position in which the young minister might have attained security and renown, for he was soon made sole pastor; yet now the enticement of security and fame could not set at rest the turbulent questions brewing in his mind, and these questions demanded some kind of answer.

There was the question of Ellen. How many times did it not recur in his early morning walks to the grave in Roxbury—in Roxbury, not so very far distant from where once he had wandered in the hills and had hoped that God and man in the bush might meet. It was inescapably true. Against that door he might beat his hands in vain. There was that which passed away and never returned. Never again could he sun himself in her eyes. The fact of outward nature, the mists of morning, the stars, all poetry—he should never again be able to connect these with the heart and life of her who had so enchanted him. And most bitter thought of all—so it seemed—was the fear that his miserable apathy might wear off, that he should resume old duties, that he should go again among friends with tranquil countenance— but no answer.

Even before Ellen's death—indeed, as early as his divinity student days, he had become progressively less satisfied with the solutions which were so neatly offered in books accepted in Cambridge. It is true that he had early been inoculated with the ideas of those hard-headed eighteenth-century philosophers whose ghosts haunted the classrooms of Harvard and pulled the puppet strings which moved the lips of the professors there. He had irritated his Aunt Mary by speaking of her beloved Wordsworth's verse as mystic and unmeaning. But when he had come upon Sampson Reed's *Growth of the Mind,* he had felt the need to ponder anew the connection of man and nature, of earth and heaven. Gradually he had seen that those cold and prudent Christians—the Bacons, Lockes, Butlers, Johnsons, Buckminsters —did not encompass all truth, but that something, too, might be said on behalf of the enthusiasts—the Pascals, the Wesleys, the Cowpers. Though truth might be known by the reason, it might also, as Pascal said, be known by the heart, and perhaps it was, after all, through the intuitions of the heart that man came to a knowledge of first principles.

In the intervals of leisure permitted by his pastorate, he had read much. He had made the acquaintance of thinkers whose ideas awakened the warmest sympathies within him, though they cut the moorings of old association and sent his thoughts far adrift upon as yet uncharted waters. It was M. De Gerando's *Histoire Comparée des Systèmes de Philosophie* which fully opened his eyes to a past of which he had been aware, but which, until now, had possessed no actual vitality.[11] Now he realized that these Greek philosophers—Anaxagoras, Pythagoras, Xenophanes, Heraclitus, and their successors—were not merely hazy figures out of a remote time, interesting, if at all, only historically, but men motivated by a living passion for knowledge, who wrestled with truth as earnestly as did any Hebrew prophet. Indeed, they had found truth—truth that was still valid. Perhaps that was the greatest service which they performed for him—to show him that men are so attuned to the order of nature that truth, truth of all kinds, is always newly available, has never been wholly confined within the covers of one book.

And then, out of that mystic cloudland of Germany, had come the writings of Goethe.[12] Whatever of shadow or of dream clung to the philosophy of his countrymen, dissolved in the bright light of Goethe's clear intellect. This man had lived deeply and intensely, and his written word pulsated as if imbued with life itself. Out of his manifold experience there had shaped itself with the clarity of the world under the midday sun the conviction that men delude themselves when they believe that God speaks to them through books and histories—that the man to whom the universe does not reveal directly what relation it has to him, whose heart does not tell him what he owes himself and others, will scarcely learn it out of books. Whatever of real inspiration, whatever of profound sentiment a man may find, he must draw from his own bosom.

These were exciting ideas which would not subside into the old calm. It was as if an inexperienced boatman, quietly resting on a lake, suddenly roused from his reverie to discover that the puff of air, the mist on the sky line, the glint of light on the water, had suddenly transformed themselves into a pattern of wind, and cloud, and lightning, and all the hazard and terror of a storm. And ye something reassuring came out of the situation. If the shore seemed hopelessly far away, and if wind and wave threatened constantly to do their very worst, nevertheless every additional new moment of life brought a new understanding of the possibilities of strength and endurance, and even a kind of disdain of the old safety.

Once having embraced these revolutionary thoughts, Emerson found it unendurable to continue living with the customary views and practices of his church. Yet the break was not an easy one. The church had provided a calling for his family for generations before him. His father had served it. Ever since his boyhood, his mother, the immediate members of his family, his friends—all had expected him to follow in his father's footsteps. He had trained himself for the ministry. A feeling for it was almost literally in his blood. And he did not want to stick at gnats—to protest unnecessarily against the forms of a relatively liberal sect. Furthermore, a break would leave him without a vocation and without a means of livelihood.

The crisis came when it did as the result of a homely situation. Some repairs being necessary to Old North and the church being closed for a time, the young minister seized the occasion to make a journey to the White Mountains in New Hampshire. There he sought the solitude which his Aunt Mary had more than once counseled as the best incentive to inspiration. At Ethan Allen Crawford's, in mid-July, he spent a cheerless Sunday, looking over the low mountains, watching the clouds covering the great peaks and obscuring the woods on the horizon. In the yard a disconsolate peacock was the only sign of animate life, and in the parlor of the inn two restless travelers were his only companions. A volume of Sewel's *History of the People Called Quakers,* containing a biographical sketch of George Fox, 'elped to occupy the slow-footed hours.[13]

The actual severing of the ties was accomplished without a display of passion. His departure from his office, the young minister said, would make no real change in his spiritual relation with his former parishioners. Whatever had been excellent in these relations was permanent, and would remain to them. The congregation, on the other hand, displayed its tolerance by continuing his salary for the time being. Within four months after his resignation, Emerson, now aged twenty-nine, broken in health again after the strain of months of perplexing thought, his young wife dead, without a vocation, and with no prospects for the future—sailed for Europe and a change of scene.

He left in a merchant vessel for Malta, and, before he had done with his travels, had visited Italy, Switzerland, France, England, and Scotland. The journey, in prospect, had interested him chiefly because it might enable him to meet face to face certain men whose writings had given him hope—Coleridge, whose wide knowledge seemed to burst the narrow boundaries of speculation and to make him a citizen of the universe; Landor, whose doctrine that the great man is he who has nothing to fear and nothing to hope from another, seemed so stimulating; Wordsworth, whose simple adherence to truth, and whose faith in his own thought, whatever the world might think, aroused one's own confidence; and lastly, Carlyle, whose love of truth and hatred of sham assured the truth-lover everywhere of sympathy.

But, on the whole, his visits with these men proved disappointing. However brilliant Landor was as a conversationalist, he was, after all, a man of whims. Coleridge was a short, thick old man who leaned on a cane, took snuff, and thereby soiled his cravat. Conversation with him was impossible. His mind moved only in its customary grooves, and could not accommodate itself to the thoughts of a new companion. Wordsworth, too, was old, a plain, white-haired man who shaded his eyes with green goggles. Though he did not speak in monologue as Coleridge did, there was a degree of peevishness in what he said. He wished that Coleridge would write more to be understood, and Carlyle he sometimes thought insane. Outside the range of his familiar thought, his opinions were of no value.

Only with the more youthful Carlyle had an exchange of ideas been really approached. Emerson had found him, tall and gaunt and lonely, in the desolate and heathery country in the parish of Dunscore. He was a voluble talker, with downright opinions when he spoke of men and things and action. But when they had gone out to walk over long hills into Wordsworth's country, and there sat themselves down and talked of the immortality of the soul, Carlyle was reluctant to speak, and their conversation came to an unsatisfactory close. It was a pity, too, it seemed to Emerson, that his friend preferred such a scrub as Mirabeau to Socrates. Though Carlyle was lovable for his love of truth, clearly he had no insight into religious truth, no comprehension of that moral truth which Emerson called the first philosophy.[14]

It was without the least sadness on that calm day in early September, that Emerson, homeward bound on the sailing vessel *New York,* saw the last hump of England receding in the distance. He was glad that his traveling was done. Now, perhaps more clearly than ever before, he recognized the apparent truth of what he had learned from the melancholy Pestalozzi—that no man in God's wide world is able to help any other man. It seemed, for a time, a rueful thought. A half-dozen years before, in those dreary months of convalescence in Florida, he had gazed over the Atlantic and mused on human mortality. Now, as the ship moved smoothly over quiet waters and under clear skies, and as he looked fixedly into the depths slipping behind him, the thought of death seemed not unpleasant. It occurred to him that he could find his way to the bottom without regret.

Such thoughts, however, were dispelled during the month-long stormy passage that followed. For days the wind howled and the ship pitched on a tempestuous sea. Conversation—any kind of recreation—was out of the question. Moreover, on such a sea, in such a wind, in such rain, on such wild, distressful, noisy nights, sleep was impossible. The cabin passengers found their sides sore with rolling in their berths. Every rope that snapped, every

spar that cracked, suggested real and imminent threat of
death, and Emerson wished himself heartily in the bushes
of Canterbury. His compassion was aroused, too, for the
steerage passengers—who comprised more than half the
thirty on shipboard—old women and children, sitting up
all night or lying in their wet berths, waiting in misery for
the distant day of landing, while the ship dived into chasms
or climbed over mountains of sea. As he lay on his berth
in the morning watch, or in periods of calm that inter-
vened between the days of storm, he came to grip, not
only with the necessity for living, but with the principles
by which, in large part, he was henceforth to live.

The problem of ascertaining the true nature of things
was made all the more difficult by the confusion of the
religionists whose very honesty obscured the partial and
imperfect character of their glimpses of the great circling
truths, which, if one could but find and state them, might
resolve one's doubts. To thrust aside that which seemed
so valuable and so wholesome to thousands of others, and
to set oneself up to expound that which was yet so incom-
pletely conceived in one's own mind, likewise made one
hesitant to question the old solutions. Nevertheless, the
charge was clear and plain for one's self, at any rate, to
formulate one's faith and to give it full obedience.

Gradually his thoughts aligned themselves into what
seemed a meaningful pattern. Beneath the welter of little,
partial versions of truth, the sectarianisms of men, is the
One Bottom of the whole law of human nature, which the
great men of all time have tried to express. It was of that
nature which Socrates and St. Bernard were speaking when
they said that a man contains within himself all that is
needful to his government, that all real good or evil that can
befall him must be from himself. A part of that One
Bottom is the truth that nothing can be given to man or

taken from him but always there is a compensation. Swedenborg was only repeating the deep insight of Plato when he asserted that there is a correspondence between the human soul and everything that exists in the world, and that the study of things, or Nature, is really an examination of that which is already within the nature of man. Goethe, too, had spoken from the depth of the Original when he had counseled to think on living—that man is to live to the real future by living to the real present, that here, in this life, are one's duties, writ as with pencil of fire. Finally, at the very heart of Truth is the highest revelation, announced by the Greek Plotinus and by the Quaker Penn, and by the Greatest One of all, that God is in every man.

VI

The places that had been dark now became light. Years before, while he was still a divinity student at Harvard, he had spoken of himself, in a moment of hypercritical self-examination, as the melancholy Jaques. However applicable then, the epithet was no longer valid, for now, in spite of a future which left uncertain many aspects of his personal fortune, he could look ahead not only with serenity, but with cheerfulness also. It was a joyous homecoming, and presently, when he had settled himself in Concord, where for two hundred years his ancestors had lived before him, all vestiges of his initial doubts and uncertainties had dropped from him. Thereafter he was essentially a man devoted to hope and forward-looking thoughts.

A SEEING EYE

For a time Emerson had contemplated building a new home on the hill across from the Old Manse—on Peter's Field, where he and his brothers had played when they had come to Concord to visit their grandfather Ezra Ripley. The spot was full of hallowed memories, new as well as old, for here he had spent many hours with Edward, the ambitious brother, now dead and buried in a lonely grave in the West Indies, and here he had walked many times with his brother Charles, who had the eye of an artist, and who pointed out things in nature which thereafter might not be seen without thought of him. Here too, as he had looked down upon the quiet river, or rambled through the adjacent woods, he had seen, in the manifold and familiar objects of the landscape, many an agreeable symbol of his thought for the little book that was now growing under his hand.

But when all was said and done, it had seemed the more practical to buy the Coolidge house on the Cambridge Turnpike just where that unfrequented road left the Great Road for Lexington and Boston. The property was without pretension or charm, though it was reputed to have the driest cellar in Concord! It stood on an acreage of lowland through which flowed Mill Brook. To the east, along the Great Road, ran some tree-covered hills, at the foot of which, beyond George Minot's place, were a number of houses, old, decrepit, and uninteresting. To the south, across Mill Brook, were more hills and woods, in the midst of which, somewhere, were several ponds, beyond which Concord River widened into Fair Haven Bay. It was, for Emerson, in those first years of his Concord residence, almost unexplored territory, wholly without endearing associations. It was toward the village proper, northward toward Sleepy Hollow, toward the Battle Ground and the river near by, that his thoughts naturally turned. There were the paths he knew. It would therefore require the planting of trees and shrubs, a garden with vegetables and flowers, the visits of friends, a good deal of family life, to remove the stiffness and strangeness of this new spot, to make it mellow and comfortable.

Who, however, could long feel strange anywhere with Charles? To have him in the new house was to bring into it at once animation and repose. What a pair of eyes he had to see! He was a born orator, too, and when he read the old Greek tragedies in the original, one perforce became enamored of the serene beauty of the Attic muse. One left then the noisy world of men, forgot Concord, forgot time, became indifferent to place.

There was Madame Emerson, too, for whom quarters were provided. She was a link with the past, a gentle reminder of a distant time, of boyhood poverty and hardship, of struggles and ambitions in college days. Her room above Waldo's study was a consecrated place where she sat much, the Book of Common Prayer, on her bureau, a kind of emblem of the Old hovering over so much here that was new.

And then there was Lidian, for whom the new house had really been obtained. One Saturday in September, he had delivered an address at Concord's celebration of its second centennial, in which he had a rightful part because of the long association of his ancestors with the village. On Monday he had driven to Plymouth, where, in the evening, he and Lidian had quietly been married. Lidian had understood about Ellen; indeed, her acceptance of his memories of Ellen had done much to make him feel so greatly at ease

in her presence. It seemed the most natural thing in the
world that they should talk of Ellen. If there was anything surprising about Lidian, it was that his thoughts were
apparently already known to her, or that they mingled so
unobtrusively with her own. She suggested deep pools and
quiet waters. He liked to call her "mine Asia." Under
her care, calm settled upon the new house. It was as if
they had always been there, as if past and present and future
had all blended into one.

II

As for friends whose visits would add warmth to the
new household, hither now had come Alcott, a consistent
idealist if ever there was one, whose *Record of a School*
aimed to show to the children the symbolical character of
all things. Here was a man who evidently wished to make
practical application of the teachings of Plato and Swedenborg. It was a very good remark in this little book, a remark
that hinted at the unity reproduced by the mind out of
several parts. True, it was perhaps only a hint, but it
touched upon something of first-rate importance, something faintly stated because dimly seen—but who had ever
fully comprehended the Idea according to which the universe is made? It was what Plato was attempting in his
Dialogues, what Goethe was struggling to express in those
fascinating poems on Metamorphosis. This tendency of
the mind to unify, to integrate particulars, to find the gen-
eralization that arranges the facts into a pattern—it is this
tendency which permits man to apprehend the law that
permeates all nature, to see that the universal law already
exists in the single fact. It is a high function of the mind
to dispel the illusion of variety, of separateness, which
follows a false devotion to facts, and to reveal the connection of all particulars in the Whole. It was a matter for

rejoicing to discover one who comprehended that the law in nature corresponds with the law in the mind of man— is perhaps only a symbol of it!

Nor was the man himself inferior to the record of his work. With him, conversation was possible. Unmistakably, he was a wise man, simple, superior to display, and dropping the best things as quietly as the least. Indeed, his spoken word seemed to show him in better light even than the *Record of a School*. It was his aim, he said, to make upon his age what impression he could through his school, in which he wrote all his thoughts; hence action through teaching, rather than speculation and writing, was his chosen field of endeavor. He thought every man a Revelation, a system, an institution, and therefore autobiography the best book. The spiritual world ought to meet men everywhere, and so the influence of Christianity should eventually actually extend into trade, government, and the arts. When he spoke, it was as Charles remarked—the conversation became nimble and buoyant, and the world began to dislimn.[1]

III

To Alcott, this first visit with Emerson at his new home in Concord was an even more auspicious occasion than it was to Emerson. Alcott was at once less self-sufficient and more demonstrative than his friend, whom nature had given a reserved temperament, and whom fortune had blessed with gifts denied to Alcott—the external assurances developed by a good formal education, the companionship of brilliant and ambitious brothers, and a tradition of family superiority, tempered, to be sure, by a dutiful sense of humility. If Emerson in these early years of his manhood was lonely, and undoubtedly he was, there were always sanctuaries, however aloof from the broad and familiar thoroughfares, to which he could retreat—cool sanctuaries where he found haven for the ultimate realities of his essentially solitary being. Alcott, on the other hand, was fundamentally of a social temperament. Without companionship, without occasion for action or opportunity for expression, he felt frustrated. He could remember desolate days in the remote time of his Philadelphia teaching when only one fellow creature (his colleague William Russell) seemed to inhabit with him the desert in which he lived. Now, in the recent period of his intellectual growth, his sense of loneliness had increased with his development. He longed for the society of an equal, for a warm companionship in which he could pour out the enthusiasms of a lively social nature, and in which his own thought might attain a greater substantiality in being welcomed by an understanding friend.

The bright October day had been an agreeable prelude to the meeting in the late afternoon. There, somewhat removed from the dust of the Great Road, stood the new house. So easily did Alcott make his entrance that it seemed he entered a house without doors. How quickly did the evening pass in conversation with Waldo and Charles and Mrs. Emerson. The next day they attended services in the old church, and Alcott sat in the family pew with Emerson and his brother. It was a scene that was to remain long in Alcott's memory—this genuine Puritan perch with the sounding board over the pulpit, these loose pew doors which rattled as the congregation rose for prayers and rattled again when the prayers were ended. Strange though it seemed, in these homely surroundings Emerson was indistinguishable from his fellow-villagers, so plain and outwardly conventional did he appear. On the Sabbath, too, Emerson had taken Alcott to the Manse, where they inspected that ancient habitation and visited with its likewise ancient inhabitant, Dr. Ripley, who warned Alcott against imbibing too deeply of the heresy of transcendentalism, though the old sage confessed that rightly he could not tell what it was!

The visit at Concord stirred Alcott's hopes as they had never been stirred before. Never had he found a man in whose whole mind he felt more sympathy, one who was scholarlike in his views and yet did not lose his humanity in his scholarship. Emerson, he thought, was one of the purest spiritualists of the day, because he comprehended, more fully than most, the presence of the Universal in man, possessed a more adequate sense of the truly Human. In spite of all his taste for Greek literature and philosophy, he was able to apprehend something genuinely spiritual behind the accumulated appendages of Christianity. It was true that in their conceptions of the life and character of Christ, Alcott discovered some disparity of idea, though he interpreted the difference as being one of association rather than of thought. It seemed to Alcott, too, that Emerson's sensitive literary taste sometimes stood in the way of his clear and hearty acceptance of the Spiritual, that his liking for artistic form occasionally meant more to him than did his love for the idea embodied in the form. But upon the whole, Alcott thought that there was a striking conformity of taste and opinion with his own.[2] At least, in communion with Emerson, his spirit had found itself—had found itself by forgetting its independent life, by losing itself in the common being of Humanity. To have such a friend was one of the rare joys and comforts of life.

Beneath these first impressions, had he been able to see deeply enough, or clearly enough, Alcott might have read much that the future had in store for his friendship with Emerson. He might have read his growing awareness of his friend's apparently meticulous care for form, a flaw which

Emerson himself, many years later, was to call one of the chief defects of Plato, a man revered by him almost above all. Alcott might have observed too, had his own convictions been plain to him, that some time long hence, in the declining days of their lives, they should approach disagreement in what he now chose to regard as a mere difference of association rather than of thought. But Alcott was still to formulate his conception of Personality, and now he was content to quiet his doubts with the obvious kinship of thought with his friend. What fate had decreed for him, and for Emerson, or what their expanding characters might create, still rested in that mysterious province which men call the future.

IV

The months that followed Alcott's first visit to Concord were felicitous beyond the common lot of men, months during which the friends experienced the rare intellectual pleasure of exploring each other's minds, exploring and finding a similarity of tastes and convictions such as both hitherto had longed for in vain. There were other visits to Concord, occasions when the growing bond of understanding and the promise of still other worlds of thought to be shared awakened a restless delight, and the whole sky was bright with hope. When Emerson came to Boston to lecture on the modern writers, there was, therefore, no more interested listener than Alcott, who recognized only a reflection of his own ideas when Emerson placed Coleridge among the sages of the world—with Plato, St. Augustine, and others sharing the clear vision of the Divinity. The eloquence of the lecturer, his sincerity, his confidence in the prospects for humanity, aroused Alcott's newly cherished hopes for the coming of a spiritual philosophy that would create a new age of thought. And Emerson came to Boston not only to lecture, but also to visit this fellow-admirer of Coleridge, this lover of Plato to whom the Dialogues were a primer of speculation and action and who employed them in his school as many a lesser teacher employed the multiplication table or the alphabet.

One of the agreeable discoveries of the friends was that each was interested in writing, not only for the mere pleasure of expression, but as a medium of influencing the conduct of the age. For some time Alcott had been working, alone, and without the aid or encouragement of anyone, on a small volume which he planned to call "Psyche, or the Breath of Childhood." It was to be an effort to unfold the spiritual agencies then at work. He drew strength for this effort from the philosophy of Coleridge and of Wordsworth, in whose essay on Epitaphs he found a satisfying explanation of the origin of the human affections. In the spirit of the sentiments of those authors, and according to his understanding of the teachings of Plato, and the sayings of Pestalozzi and Jesus concerning infancy, did Alcott labor to embody his thoughts in the "Breath of Childhood." And less formally, indeed, partly in preparation for "Psyche," he recorded his reflections in his diary, upon which he worked with great care. A smaller project, something to reveal the practical application of his ideas in his teaching, was the *Record of Conversations,* which, unlike "Psyche," saw the light of day in print.

Emerson, too, had for several years been working on a little book, the earliest plans for which had occurred to him in the first quiet days at sea after he had bid the shores of England an unreluctant farewell. Then, when he had come with his mother and brother Charles to make his home with his step-grandfather, his plans became clearer, and the pages grew. The presence of Charles was a lively stimulus, many a thought flowing from his conversation, and many an image suggesting itself as he pointed out objects in the rural Concord scene. The pink ribbons of clouds in the winter sunset were to Charles like goldfishes floating in a sea of crimson light—that, and something more. Had they no expression? What was it that Nature would say? With such prompting from the beloved brother, the thoughts for the chapter on Beauty shaped themselves for the little book. It was a task simple and pleasing—scarcely a task at all—to record such thoughts, to the accompaniment, perhaps, of a surly storm that thickened the night and rocked the walls of the Manse, and blew through its chinks and cracks. Outside, the great willow over the roof caught the wind and trumpeted every caprice of the gods. Sometimes it seemed that *Nature* was almost writing itself.

When the friendship with Alcott had begun, there had begun, too, an exchange of manuscripts. Though the *Conversations* were for the public eye, the pages of Alcott's diary had been for himself alone, and Alcott had known of none to whom he might confide the cherished "Psyche." Now, however, the diary and "Psyche," as well as the *Conversations,* came naturally into Emerson's hands, and at the very time that his own first book was taking form.[3]

For Emerson it was a joyful discovery to find in the Alcott papers his own thoughts, thoughts which had been recurring more and more frequently in the past few years, and which, now, in the writings of his friend, clarified and crystallized as never before. Ideas from Swedenborg and his disciple Sampson Reed, which Emerson had found kindred to his own, now seemed as solid as the land in Massachusetts, as they came to him again in the manuscripts of this reader and lover of Plato—Plato, who had anticipated the best of Swedenborg long ago. In these manuscripts of his friend he found many of the theses which he was incorporating in his own book. The distinction between the idealist and the spiritualist, that matter is but the form and shadow of spirit (the foundations of man are not in matter but in spirit), that spirit loses somewhat in its incarnation (a man is a god in ruins), that science, with its emphasis on analysis, sees only a partial picture, and therefore beholds a seemingly disconnected world (the reason why the world lacks unity, and lies broken and in heaps, is because man is disunited with himself), and that nature is, in short, an emblem of the soul (every object, rightly seen, unlocks a new faculty of the soul)—these ideas and others Emerson found in the written and the spoken words of his friend, as Alcott was aware, and as Emerson himself acknowledged in the summarizing "Prospects" in *Nature*, the words, he said, sung to him by a certain poet. The service thus given in solidifying Emerson's thought was a debt which Emerson never forgot, though he was yet to know Alcott almost fifty years, during some of which the bonds of friendship were sorely to be strained. But it was a firm belief with Emerson that sublimity can scarcely be better attained than by keeping one's obligations across the years.

When the published *Nature* finally came into his possession, a gift to the author, Alcott very modestly entered in his diary a note recording his participation in the writing—that Mr. Emerson had adverted, indirectly, to his "Psyche," then in Emerson's hands.[4] No more. He thought of Emerson as one of whom the age was not worthy, as one unrivaled among American writers. And Emerson was his friend.

v

No single project, save his diary, occupied so much of Alcott's energy as did his "Psyche, or the Breath of Childhood," for no subject, during the years of his early maturity, was so dear to him as childhood. Childhood was the little field which he proposed to cultivate as his part in the introduction of a new and better era. What Wordsworth had said about the divine nature of the child, suggested to Alcott a deep if impenetrable truth. Jesus' saying, "Suffer the little children to come unto me, for of such is the kingdom of heaven," was to Alcott no mild approbation of the merely engaging manners of childhood. It was, on the contrary, a very serious saying, which, when understood in its true sense, would regenerate the present system of education and society. The child's joyous yearning for the beautiful, its trust in human sayings, its deep love for those on whom it relies for attention and support, its picturing of ideal life, its simplicity, its freedom from prejudice and false sentiment—surely these things hinted some superiority not to be seen in the dim nature of the adult and worldly man?

It was during the first winter of this intimate acquaintance that Alcott drew together his courage and asked Emerson to read and criticize his manuscript copy of "Breath of Childhood." He was interested in Emerson's comment, not only because Emerson was his friend, but chiefly because he knew of no one among his contemporaries who had a richer judgment or a purer taste, or who had a greater power of thought or more success in expression than Emerson. Hitherto he had been left to find his own manner, to form his own style—indeed, to proceed alone without encouragement of any kind. To be able to give his manuscript into the hands of so valuable a critic and so warm a friend seemed to Alcott a stroke of fortune.

A month elapsed before Emerson returned the manuscript. His criticisms Alcott found encouraging, though they were a mingling of praise and censure. Alcott was quite willing to confess that what he had written had but a general unity, knit loosely together by threads of association felt only by himself, and that his little book revealed but fitful glimmerings of an idea scarcely mastered, and dwelt upon to diffuseness. That it was a book of strong mannerisms, that it was deficient in variety of thought and illustration—these and the other judgments of his friend Alcott readily accepted as true. It was enough for him to realize that in Emerson's view he had not wholly failed of success. It was no small thing to know that Emerson thought his book original and vital in all its parts, and written so as to awaken the apprehension of the Absolute. What greater praise could he wish than to be told that his book left him no liberty to neglect or conceal his gifts as a writer?

Spring had come, and midsummer, before Alcott ventured once more to leave with Emerson a revised "Breath of Childhood," which he now called, simply, "Psyche." Emerson was busy during these summer days adding more pages to his own *Nature*. Charles had died in May, and Emerson had bravely commemorated his passing in the final page on Discipline. With Charles gone, it was more than ever pleasant to have these visits from Alcott and to listen to his Olympian dreams. His "Psyche" was an excellent stimulus to thought, difficult though it might be to criticize. It was December before Emerson returned the manuscript. In the meanwhile he had thought of it often— had showed it to Elizabeth Hoar, the wise and gentle Elizabeth who was to have married Charles, and who was as a sister now to Waldo. They had agreed that Alcott should publish.

But in the meanwhile Alcott had had certain experiences which made him skeptical of the wisdom of any further attempt at writing and publishing and which threatened to destroy the entire pattern of his life. The publication of his *Conversations with Children on the Gospels,* which Emerson had read so sympathetically, pulled down upon Alcott's head violent charges of absurdity, of obscenity, of blasphemy.

In vain did Emerson endeavor to obtain for his friend a favorable hearing. The public press of Boston was aroused. Alcott was convinced that his school must fail, the school through which he had hoped to act in preparation for the new age. It was, beyond question, a crucial moment in his life, though he was as yet only partially conscious of the doubt and the threat of despair that the future held in store for him.

Only Emerson, thought Alcott, understood him, and he, only in part. Emerson counseled giving up teaching. In the thick of the storm of abuse, he had written a calm and friendly letter in which he urged what he called his golden view of his friend—that Alcott leave the impractical world to wag its own way, and sit apart and write his oracles for its behoof. It would be preferable, he said, to choose some manual or quite mechanical labor as a means of living that should leave a few sacred hours in the twenty-four, to any attempts to realize a cherished idea in any existing intellectual or spiritual forms, when by defying every settled usage in society he should be sure to sour his own temper.

Emerson's advice awoke again in Alcott's mind the uncertainties with which he had struggled long ago in the bleak years of his solitude and self-education. Should he concern himself with practical action or should he devote himself to speculation? Emerson, thought Alcott, valued his friend's professional labors—his teaching—somewhat too low, while, as a writer, he overestimated his ability. Still, Emerson might be right; perhaps the speculative element rather than the practical did predominate in his nature. It was a perplexing question, though beneath his doubts Alcott sensed an irrepressible instinct to act, and without finding scope for the exercise of his instinct he felt restless and unfulfilled. To see his Idea merely a written word could give him no abiding peace; it must likewise be a spoken and an acted word. What he had once written, and what Emerson himself had once approved, was for him, at least, irrevocably true: Nothing is complete until it is enacted.

VI

The decision to oppose his friend's advice was to Alcott not an easy choice. To follow it would have been to yield to an old leaning toward a speculative life, and what was to follow, temporarily, the line of least resistance. This clash of wills and personalities led Alcott to a closer scrutiny of his friend than his enthusiasms had hitherto permitted. Perhaps his desire to express an independent judgment caused him somewhat to overshoot his mark. There may have been in his attitude somewhat of the exaltation and fine frenzy that are a part of martyrdom, for, in a sense, a martyr Alcott certainly was. At any rate, he entered now in his diary a criticism of Emerson which, if excessive in his calmer view, nevertheless struck off some convictions that he was to harbor in one form or another for many years and that he was to hold most firmly as the passing decades brought a fulfillment, in altered guise, of these ambitions of the late morning of his life.

He had spent several days in Concord to escape from the vexations of public calumny and the cares of a dwindling school, and to discuss with Emerson what Alcott called the means and methods of communicating with the age. He had returned to Boston, not cheered and refreshed as he had hoped, but saddened, and, as he then thought, disillusioned with his friend. It appeared now that Emerson as a writer held men and things at a distance, pleasing himself by using them for his own benefit, as a means of gathering material for his works. He seemed not to believe in the actual, in the human, for its own sake. His sympathies were all intellectual. He idealized all things, and this idealized picture was to him the real and the true. Even persons he thus idealized, and his interest in them, and their influence over him, ceased when this conformity no longer appeared in his imagination. Beauty, beauty it was that charmed him. All that distorted beauty, however good or true, was of no interest to his mind. It was not so much the desire of being holy and true that drew him on, as the desire to set forth in fit and graceful terms the beauty of truth and holiness. His mission was to give pleasure more than to impart truth. As a man, he seemed not quite in earnest. It was, after all, for effect that he wrote and spoke, fame standing before him as a dazzling award. His life had been one of opportunity, and he had sought to realize in it more of the accomplished scholar than of the perfect man. He was an eye rather than a heart, an intellect rather than a soul. The intellectual pursuit of the esthetic—this was the quest with which he was really engrossed.[5]

Though Emerson was unaware of the refinements of his friend's criticisms, he sensed the presence of a barrier— knew that, in spite of efforts at practical aid, he had failed to resolve Alcott's dilemma. The three days of Alcott's visit at Concord had found Emerson lumpish, tardy, and apathetic, by reason of a bad cold. Yet he felt keenly and more certainly than ever before that Alcott was the most extraordinary man and the highest genius of the time, one who was erect, who saw truly, and who was content with nothing less than a present life freed from all taint of the forms of the past. With Alcott's proposal to expand his effort of talking with schoolteachers and holding con- versations in the villages to spread his educational ideas, he even agreed, though he hesitated to counsel so novel an experiment. But the uniformity of Alcott's mind he con- fessed he found monotonous—the incessant search for truth and the origin of things, the refusal to be amused, the indifference toward the merely pleasant. It was sad that there could be between them only a partial meeting of minds, that they could touch only at points. When he had considered the hindrances to a oneness of thought with Carlyle, it had seemed that it was sea and poverty and pursuit that held them apart; yet now the imperfect union with Alcott made it clear that he and Alcott— and all men, indeed—were insular, were infinitely repellant orbs, holding their undivided beings on that condition. At the last— they would be, for ever, balked souls!

Alcott's conviction that Emerson's primary interests lay in intellect and in beauty may be one of the major criticisms to which Emerson's thought is subject, so largely do these Hellenic traits bulk among his expressions. The criticism was of a kind with Emerson's own of Plato—that the screaming Hebrew prophets were in a way more convincing than the polished and literary founder of the Academy. No one, however, was more convinced than Emerson that character is higher than intellect. The emphasis upon the intellectual and the esthetic which to Alcott now seemed so overwhelming was in part an illusion occasioned by the mountains high and rivers wide which divide even those most fully in accord. Alcott was simply unaware that Emerson, who was endeavoring so ineffectually to understand and to assist his friend, had his own difficulties, of which he had not spoken to Alcott, and which he was trying in his own way to solve.

The panic of 1837, with the closing of the Boston banks and the bankruptcy of many apparently substantial merchants, was not without effect upon Emerson's modest fortune. His one published book had brought him no returns, and the income from his lectures was as yet negligible. Those unspeakably pleasant days in mid-May, when Alcott had visited him, were full of an unvoiced uncertainty and apprehension. What was there that a scholar could do to change the face of things? Therefore he busied himself, planting trees about his house, pines and chestnuts, stirring the earth about his shrubs, and walking in the woods and pastures, following the bumblebee and the pine warbler, and listening to the Maryland yellow-throats and the bobolinks. When it was impossible to be a doer, it might still be possible to be a spectator. A man should be able to ride more than one horse. When action is denied, the enjoyment of beauty yet remains to make life sweet until another day. So he found the yellow-breeched philosopher, the bumblebee, who sees only what is fair, wiser far than the human seer who is obsessed by want and woe.

That he basked in beauty Emerson freely admitted; but that he stopped there, as his friend in his own troubled days unhappily feared, he never himself would have agreed. He was inspired with a greater ambition to conquer in his own person every calamity by understanding it and its cause. He wished to live with a belief that a perfect insight of a disaster is an everlasting deliverance from its fear.[6] But a warmer Alcott was perhaps right. It was through intellect that Emerson hoped that character might be attained. His was the Socratic view that knowledge is virtue. With this view, Alcott, in spite of his love for Plato and the Neoplatonists, never felt entirely at home. As the years came upon him, the emphasis on intellect which he found in Hellenism appealed to him less and less. More and more he found comfort in the Hebraic ideals of faith and obedience, though at the end he was to confess the difficulty of making a firm and exclusive choice. The difference between the two friends was, however, a real one. It was, perhaps, a matter of temperament, which to

Emerson always remained one of the darkest mysteries of Nature.

VII

But the friendship did not cease. The eddy quietly spent its force, and the wind soon blew again in its accustomed direction, with no other immediate effect than to hint the course of future currents. Nor did the friends cease to discuss Alcott's prospects; nor did Alcott at once decide to abandon all writing. "Psyche" he kept beside him, even when public criticism of him was at its worst and when failure and poverty most darkly threatened. From time to time he revised what he had written or added to the pages of his little book.

He was encouraged to continue with his writing by Emerson's offer to pay for the publication of "Psyche." Emerson had already published Carlyle's *Sartor Resartus,* and was now bringing out his *French Revolution.* To Alcott the offer was very welcome, for the publication of his *Conversations* had been a financially unprofitable venture, and his present want made impossible any expenditures save those for the immediate needs of his family. Though Emerson asked that "Psyche" appear at once, Alcott pleaded for a delay of several months for further revision. The idea which he wished to embody in "Psyche" was to Alcott one of the greatest import. He doubted that he had done justice to his subject, and he hesitated to send his book into the light of day misshapen or prematurely born.

Then, after months had passed and Alcott had left his manuscript for his friend's final judgment, Emerson returned the sheets with the advice that, after all, "Psyche" be not published.[7] Though Alcott himself had hesitated to proceed with his writing, and though he agreed to the wisdom of Emerson's final advice that the book be not pub-

lished, the effect upon him was after all one of discourage-
ment. He despaired almost of ever writing anything worthy
of himself. It lamed him to think that though he felt himself commanded to speak, he yet had no voice. A year had
come and gone before he again permitted himself to believe
that some day his thought would receive proper expression,
and that then it might flow in another and deeper channel.
But it was not until years afterward, when he had attained
success in another field and when he had freed himself
from the overshadowing influence of his friend, that he
returned again to publish. "Psyche," however, though revised many times and at last copied in Alcott's most careful
and loving hand, seemed fated for ever to remain among
the unborn.

VIII

Such near-frustrations, such loneliness of spirit, such
dull, chill November days, were for Alcott, nevertheless, not
without alteration, not without new hopes for as yet un-
experienced ventures in friendship, for promises of a future
bright and warm and congenial to an ever-widening vista
of cheerful thought. There were even times when his
fleeting doubts, aroused by what seemed Emerson's teaching of the absolute impersonality of the soul, dissolved
wholly, so that his mind appeared to merge fully with his
friend's. At such times it was with joy that he defended
Emerson, as well as himself, against the charges of George
Ripley and others who felt that the denial of personality
was virtually a denial of God, a species of atheism. This
charge of impiety only made firmer his sense of kinship
with Emerson, setting them apart, he thought, from those
who had not yet seen into the depths of the soul. Indeed,
the obloquy which he and Emerson had had heaped upon
them made him all the more confident that a new age of

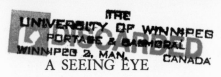

thought was dawning, an age in which the grounds of
human faith would be re-examined, the soul explored in all
its deep and mystic facts, and theology, no longer resting
on the dead letter of tradition, assume the form of a science.
Central in this new age of thought would be the idea already presented by Emerson in his public lectures in Boston,
the doctrine of the immutability and retribution of the
moral sense, that is, the divinity of the will, the gospel
which it is always publishing in the heart—its supremacy
to nature and to time.

It was in Emerson that Alcott chiefly rested his hopes
for a regeneration of thought in America. In Emerson he
saw almost the only instance in our country of a scholar
devoted, not only to authorship, but to high culture—a
genius of Olympian order, the wisest man of his day. The
increasing attendance at Emerson's lectures of so many
young people in audiences such as might be found nowhere
else on this side the Atlantic was to Alcott one of the noble
facts of the time. It was true that occasionally, in these
lectures, Emerson revealed his limitations, as when, in his
lecture on comedy, his theory and instances sparkled with
wit, cold and intellectual, but were devoid of humor, the
genial and kindly feeling of the heart. If Emerson should
fail, it would be, doubtless, because of his passionless temperament and his deficiency of stern discipline. It remained
to be seen whether he possessed that persistency of will
which vanquishes the hindrances of fortune. But insight
he unquestionably had, and Alcott looked to him to act
on the minds of those who were to bring about the new age.

IX

It was, then, as a thinker rather than as a doer, that
Alcott regarded Emerson, and though Alcott himself often
wished to devote his energies to action, it was to a life of

thought that his genius held him. There was little opportunity for action in the duties of a teacher of a private
elementary school, especially when his school was dwindling
to the vanishing point! Nor was Emerson's life that of a
man of affairs. On Sundays he had been driving with
horse and buggy to preach in a number of villages near
Concord, chiefly in East Lexington, where, in a little upstairs hall, he met a struggling congregation who found it
too far to walk to the more prosperous and more fashionable
church in West Village. His small income thus earned,
Emerson supplemented more and more by lectures, in Boston at first, and then elsewhere. So his days passed quickly
enough, though his vocation led him deeper and deeper into
study and meditation. Therefore in the friendship of Emerson and Alcott, as in their callings, especially in these earlier
years, there was little bustle or stir, nothing externally dra-
matic. They met in Boston or Concord, they walked, they
talked; they lived for the most part a life of the mind.

At his retired home in Concord, conveniently removed
from the noise and the disturbing social life of Boston, and
yet not too far away for an occasional journey to the city,
Emerson took increasing pleasure in solitary walks among
the rural scenes near the village. In these years he still
walked much on the hills opposite his house, on those hills
on the southern slopes of which the first settlers had dug
their homes. In the spring the new brown of the hillsides
tempted him among the snow banks to see whether his
wood alleys were open, though sometimes he retreated when
he found that too much winter remained. More often he was
now venturing toward Walden Pond, where the flying
clouds and Walden Woods were more remote from society.
(Poor Society! the woods seemed to say.) Sometimes, with
Henry Thoreau, he walked even beyond Walden to the
cliffs, where, on a warm spring day, the great mountain

amphitheater seemed to drink with gladness the pleasant, misty atmosphere. In that solitude a crow's voice filled the miles of air with sound, and made the world friendly and companionable. In the wood, God was manifest. In the cathedral larches the ground-pine crept him, the thrush sang him, the wild apple bloomed him. In such scenes it was easy to see and to yield one's self to the perfect whole.

There were walks at night, too, with varying results. At ten, as he worked over his dreamy journal, the moon rose behind the pointed pines in the distant woods and tempted him abroad into the bright light. Though the full moon in the clouds struck him with poetic wonder as he stepped from his warm house into the chill, grand, instantaneous night, the charm which floated and danced before him vanished only too soon. In an instant all human associations were left behind—wife and mother and child— and he was alone with the primeval elements—water, air, light, carbon, lime, granite. About him the frogs might pipe, waters tinkle far off, or grass bend and rustle; he himself had died out of the human world and had come to feel a strange, cold, ethereal, unsatisfying existence. At other times, more agreeably, he walked under the stars through the snow, stopping now and then to look at those far sparklers and to listen to the wind. It was as if the voice of the wind, so slight and pure and deep, were the sound of the stars revolving. The wonder and meaning of these stars seemed inexhaustible, these points of light which addressed the imagination and the interrogating soul, speaking, asking, warning. Better still were the spring and summer nights when the moon made amber of the world, and the meadows sent up rank smells of ferns and grasses and flowers, and the little harlot flies of the lowlands sparkled in the grass and air. It was all music. In these divine pleasures of walks on a June night under the moon and stars, he could be as a spectator of his life, standing aloof from its honor and shame. The dusty old road past his house, a road so tedious and homely by day, on such nights became Italy or Palmyra. On such nights, when the moon broke out of the clouds, his thoughts rushed forth too. It seemed clear that one who had seen such beauty had been present, too, at the creation of light and of the world; that he who had been in love had assisted at a new and second morning; and that he who through weary experience of sweet and smart had attained character, had beheld, also, a greater and worthier creation.[8]

x

Into such rural scenes, among Emerson's favorite haunts, Alcott gradually made his way. Though he had been a great stimulus to his friend in the writing of *Nature,* and though he believed devoutly in the symbolical and provocative character of nature, yet his mind dwelt with the term in its general application rather than with what Emerson called the essences unchanged by man. The city, other men, and books chiefly charmed Alcott and awakened his thoughts. It was not until his school had broken up, after Boston had proved finally inhospitable to his ideas, and until he had sought refuge and vocation in Concord near Emerson, that nature in the common sense really came to attract him. In later years the Concord River, Walden Pond, and the changing seasons were to be very dear to him; but he was perhaps never the walker that Emerson was, nor the lover of solitude.

It was in Boston that the friends generally met in these last years of Alcott's teaching. Emerson came up not infrequently to lecture, to read in the Athenaeum, or to visit the art galleries. At the Athenaeum they might retire to the privacy of one of the upper rooms to discuss such com-

mon interests as the success of Carlyle's *French Revolution,*
published in America at Emerson's risk, the early sale of
eight hundred copies having warranted the venture. Or
Emerson would come to spend an hour or two at Alcott's
house of a morning or an afternoon. At such times Emerson
might speak of his plans for new lectures, or the friends
would review again the storm aroused by Emerson's
Divinity School *Address.* The articles in the English journals
came in for their share of the conversation, and the prospect
of an American magazine worthy to express the sentiments
of the new age. Emerson spoke hopefully of a new poetry,
of a new poem of the soul which, by the excess of its spiritual
glory, would cast a shadow on all poetry of the past. There
were walks to Munroe's, where some of the new books were
examined, and where, one day, Emerson gave Alcott a copy
of Carlyle's *Miscellanies,* a rich contribution, Alcott thought,
to English literature. Sometimes they entertained themselves by exchanging lists of the names of the truly great
men of the world. On one such occasion Emerson scribbled
his list in pencil on a scrap of paper which Alcott approving-
ly pasted into his diary. The list is an epitome of the
minds of the friends: Pythagoras, Heraclitus, Zoroaster,
Confucius, Jesus, Plato, Socrates, Plotinus, Bruno, Boehme,
Swedenborg. But in his own diary Emerson confessed
that if he were pressed sternly, his list for the day must
be limited to two—Jesus and Shakespeare, representatives,
respectively, of the moral sentiment and of the beauty of the
world, of love, and of wisdom.[9]

Some of their best meetings, however, occurred on the
evenings after Emerson had spoken in Boston, when, the
lecture done, Emerson walked with Alcott to the latter's
home. Here, fired by a common train of thought awakened
by the lecture, their minds moved most closely together,
their awareness of mutual regard became most lively, the

exchange of confidences most easy and complete. What it was in Emerson's address on prudence that stirred them both, if indeed it was something in the address or the circumstances of its delivery, remains untold; but on that January night there was a conversation memorable to them both, and perhaps far-reaching in its consequences for Alcott. After the lecture Emerson had come to spend the evening with Alcott until ten o'clock, and then Alcott had accompanied his friend to his lodging. They had spoken of Alcott's plans of journeying through towns and villages, teaching and preaching the new doctrines and disciplines of culture. Emerson had been reluctant to advise in an undertaking without precedent, though he counseled that every new mind ought to take the attitude of Columbus—put behind him the ignorance of the old and sail west for a new world. Then it was, as they threaded their way along the dark Boston streets to Emerson's quarters, that their minds met in a harmony as perfect as any they were probably ever to experience. He knew of no man, said Emerson of his friend, of diviner faith in the soul, or who, amidst every hindrance, stood so firmly by it as Alcott. If he would only abide by himself, the world would come round to him at last.

It was a high compliment that Emerson was paying to his friend, for he was telling him that in him he was seeing the realization of a principle exemplified also in the lives of some whom Emerson regarded as the greatest men of modern times—Luther, Goethe, and Wordsworth—all of whom had obeyed their genius against the judgment and scorn of the world. In his own private thought, it is true, Emerson sometimes agreed with Margaret Fuller that Alcott was one-toned, though he stood ready to defend Alcott against charges of a centralism akin to that of common monomaniacs, for Alcott, he maintained, looked with wise love at all real facts, was no dodger of significant reality. He was underestimated because he could hear the voice which had said to George Fox, "That which others trample on must be thy food." He had more faith in the ideal than anyone in Emerson's acquaintance; he was a fortification against the materialism and unbelief of his times. He did not need to be learned, he was so discerning of truth. And not the least of his virtues was the fact that he was the most majestic converser whom Emerson met. In his presence, more than in that of any other, Emerson had leave to be, could see most clearly the course of his own thought.[10]

XI

But during these apparently halcyon days, beneath these felicities of friendship, there were subterranean rumblings to remind the friends that they walked the earth as ordinary mortals do, that however much they loved to dwell with the ideal, there remained always an irreducible element of earthly experience. The problem was somewhat less acute for Emerson, because Fortune, if she had not embraced him with a hearty gesture, had not recently threatened to desert him wholly. He had known sleepless nights and worried days in those months of country-wide financial panic, and there was a time after his Divinity School address when the stern old war-gods of Boston and Cambridge had shaken their heads and muttered maledictions which threatened to ruin his reputation and to make a livelihood through lecturing impossible. But these storms he weathered, not without anxiety, though with no despair.

It was Alcott who was fated to carry the heavier burden. In his philosophically formative years he had struggled to find the nexus between the physical and the spiritual philosophy; now he groped in worldly darkness seeking to link the theoretical with the practical, to find, not only a vocation, but a means of livelihood to provide the simplest necessities of life. His beautiful Temple School had long since been closed and its appointments seized to satisfy his creditors. Presently he brought to a close also the classes for a handful of children whom he had instructed in his own home. He was deeply in debt and without source of income. His family was in actual want.

If his gifts had been those of an ordinary man, or if he could have been content with subsistence merely, his situation would have been much less extreme. But his mind dwelt less upon the physical needs of his household than upon his eagerness to participate in what he called the grand revision of the thought of his age. It was his faith that if he could but find an adequate means for expressing the spirit which prompted him, the worldly needs, as Jesus had said, would take care of themselves. In this conviction he had spoken to Emerson of his intention to teach and preach in the adjacent towns and villages. It seemed, indeed, a novel plan, but then Emerson was apparently making a success of the new scheme of lecturing from town to town, a scheme which permitted him to say on weekdays what he might not say from the pulpit on Sundays, and which was more and more promising a satisfactory livelihood; hence Alcott's plan seemed not altogether unfeasible. Alcott's intention, however, was not to deliver formal addresses, but to lead in dialogues or conversations in a circle of congenial minds.

His precedent he found in his favorite readings—in the New Testament and in the writings of Plato. The practice of Socrates to teach through the medium of conversation was to Alcott the highest recommendation of the method. Jesus, too, was a perfect master of the art of conversing, which was seemingly his chosen organ of communication with men—John, especially, having recorded some perfect specimens of the master's skill. This lost art Alcott would revive and prove its primary place in the means of culture. To such labors of high colloquy he wished to devote himself exclusively.

Perhaps in these early ventures Alcott had not yet fully developed his technique; perhaps he was not yet in complete command of his own convictions; or perhaps he was too near home, too near people who could see only the ostracized, poverty-stricken schoolmaster and not the natural-born teacher, the man to whom right thought was dearer than bread and life itself. Years later, after many futile efforts, after want and despondency had done their worst with him, he was to attain an expert mastery of his medium, an audience, and—at last—remuneration; but now only a handful attended his conversations, though the growing needs of his family did not cease.

What brought him nearest to despair was the persuasion that he was not in true relation to his time. He suffered daily and deeply for sympathy, for society, for a fit exercise of his faculties. And yet an instinct for action so lively as his must find its organ by and by. Something for him to do, something adapted to his genius, Providence must have! But, in the meanwhile, how wide the distance between his actual and his ideal! And in his difficulty he seemed utterly alone; only of his own heart could he take counsel, for no one entered into his purpose, none could help or advise. In the depths of his bitterness, it appeared to him that none of his friends had sufficient insight to apprehend the justice of his life with regard to his attitude toward making a living. All thought him false to his family, dishonest in his transactions with the world. In theory, they agreed with him as

to the beauty and supremacy of wisdom—its self-sufficiency;
that its lovers should subsist upon it, and abide by its law.
But when he endeavored to put his faith into practice, they
raised an outcry against him! Speculatively, men might
believe in wisdom and sing her praises, but few, it seemed,
were willing to love and serve her without recompense. It
was no easy thing to abide by one's self while one waited
for the world to come round to one at last.

While he was thus staring into this black and bottomless
pit, Alcott received an invitation to dine with Emerson and
Nathaniel Frothingham and Margaret Fuller at George Ban-
croft's, an invitation which he declined with unspoken
words as harsh as any he ever permitted himself even in his
inmost thoughts. The frenzy which is a part of the sense of
martyrdom and of despair, seized him again. Was it, he
confided to his diary, a proper place for him at the tables
of the fashionable, the voluptuous, the opulent? Was he
not rather a present and living rebuke to all such? What
had he to do among the Sadducees? He felt too deeply the
injustice of his townsmen to sit in their midst as a guest,
fed by their charity and receiving his standing in society
from their favor.

And so, on a mid-December afternoon of 1839, the proud
idealist, instead of dining at his ease, trudged among the
machine shops of Boston, making inquiries concerning the
wages of labor. Sternly he tried to assure himself that
penury is a ministry of blessing to the soul, and has its reve-
lations in store for the patient and the meek, who, amidst
destitution, possess the earth and are also denizens of heaven.
Years later there was in the Alcott family a favorite household saying—"Poor as poverty, but serene as heaven." He
had not yet attained that calm altitude; but he was certainly on his way up into the mountain.[11]

Though Emerson was not unaware of these grim wres-
tlings of his friend, he was unable to aid him as he would.
In his own somewhat similar crisis, when he had been trying to arrive at first principles, he had reflected, with
Pestalozzi, that there are times when no man can help
another. Moreover, it was one of his limitations, he remembered, to be a seeing eye rather than a helping hand. In
facing his own problems, it had long been his conviction
that a calamity is already largely conquered when one
understands its causes. As he regarded Alcott's difficulty,
this intellectual detachment, this impersonal insight, came
into play, too. When he commended an adroit New York
broker to Alcott, it was with some amusement that he received Alcott's rebuke that he—Alcott—had the greater
austerity and that he received with reluctance the hand of
a mere merchant or banker. Nothing seemed more comic
to Emerson than the mutual condescension with which
Alcott and the wealthy Colonel Perkins shook hands. Alcott
with his hatred of labor and his commanding contemplation
was indeed a haughty beneficiary. He was a kind of stylite,
like Simeon of Antioch, perched on a pillar high and un-
comfortable above the minor vanities of the world. On
the other hand, Emerson recognized that the private soul
may ascend to transcendental virtue, that, specifically, Alcott
was without apparent injustice in refusing to pay a debt so
long as he remained in his trance, kept true to his principles.
He regularly contributed funds to what he called Alcott's
theophilanthropic school, discussed with him many times
the manifold angles of Alcott's problems, and assured him
of a warm welcome should he decide to simplify his lot
by removing to Concord, where he might live very inex-
pensively, and perhaps receive a few children into his home

as boarders and pupils. Frequently, quietly, and unobtrusively Emerson did what he could to aid his friend. What
Alcott really needed, Emerson saw, was a pure success. If
those whose opinion was fame could only see him as he
really was, could only heartily express their joy in his best
virtues, his genius would be relieved of those spots with
which a sense of injustice and loneliness had shaded it.[12]
But it was one thing thus to diagnose so accurately; it was
quite another to provide a remedy. Whatever of success
Alcott was to attain, was as yet in the remote future. It
was to come through channels as yet not dreamed of.

THE QUEST OF THE ABSOLUTE

IN THE PUBLIC FUROR that had followed the publication of the *Conversations with Children on the Gospels,* Emerson had advised his friend to engage in some quite simple manual labor as a means of earning a living in preference to a task which required a defiance of public opinion and might result in a souring of his own temper. Of this advice and of Emerson's invitation that he come to live among the simplicities of rural Concord, Alcott now bethought himself. Therefore in the spring of 1840 he removed with his family from Boston to the western outskirts of Concord village, a little beyond the river, and there occupied the Hosmer cottage, with its large garden, its acre of ground, and open fields on three sides. It was only a mile or so from Emerson's house. Although it was unpretentious, it was a pretty cottage, Alcott thought, and he became attached to it. Years later his famous daughter threw over it a glow of sentiment, called it the "Dove-cote," Meg's first home, a little brown house with a lawn "about as big as a handkerchief." But now the little women were still very small: Louisa eight, Anna nine, and Elizabeth five. May was born here several months after the family arrived.

Alcott was trying to make his living by working for hire among his Concord neighbors—in the fields behind a plow, in the woodlots with his axe. Emerson, in spite of his own counsel, dared hardly hope for his friend's success in an adventure so remote from his recent habits. Besides, he felt that Alcott had not yet brought himself to a full realization of what every young farmer recognized—that he must depend on himself, that he could never plan well while he still looked for aid from others. Moreover, it was, thought Emerson, an excessive refinement of sensibility on Alcott's part to distrust his new undertaking simply because he found it a very popular step, approved by merchants and brokers, a class of people whom Alcott did not care to please. But it was nevertheless cheering to find Alcott nailing down carpets in his new home and buying gardening tools for his new tasks. For the first time in years Mrs. Alcott went singing about the house.

For all that he was now ostensibly a village laborer, Alcott's intellectual interests did not cease. Even before his removal to Concord, he had shared the enthusiasm of his friends in their plans for a new journal to give expression to the thoughts which agitated their circle. He had felt the need for such an organ inasmuch as none of the existing magazines sufficiently recognized the rising idealistic tendency of the age. The *Christian Examiner,* which New England had once read with a conviction that it was in the vanguard of thought, he regarded as timid and conservative. The *Liberator,* true enough, had its roots in the soul. However, even Brownson's *Boston Quarterly Review,* the best journal current this side of the Atlantic, fell far below the idea of the best minds in America. Yes, Alcott would welcome a better publication. Indeed, it was he who had christened the new journal the *Dial,* the title which he had given his own beloved diary. Now that his friends, Margaret Fuller and Emerson, were actually gathering matter for the first number, his interest grew, especially since he himself was being asked to contribute.

It was at Emerson's instance that some of Alcott's "Orphic Sayings" appeared in the initial number of the *Dial.* In offering them to Margaret Fuller, Emerson recognized that they labored with Alcott's inveterate faults of being cold, vague generalities, though they were better than he

feared. They would pass muster, he thought, and might
be considered just and great. He advised that, contrary to
the intended general practice of the *Dial,* Alcott's name be
written out in full over the "Sayings," for then those who
knew Alcott would have his voice in their ears whilst they
read, and to them, at least, his words would have a majestic
sound. When the first issue had actually come from the
press, and Emerson had had an opportunity to see the *Dial*
in the body, it was Alcott's contribution that he regarded of
outstanding importance, for it seemed to him that there
was little else in the new journal, including his own offerings, that might not appear in any other periodical.[1]

Emerson might well esteem the "Orphic Sayings" as he
did. They were the fruit of long years of Alcott's reading,
his teaching, his contemplation, his adversity, and they
reflected many of Emerson's own favorite ideas. Here, if
anywhere, was the new spiritual thought, the new American
transcendentalism, its origins resting not in Kant, who had
given the name, but in the Platonists and the Christian
mystics. Here, distilled from the best of his insight, was
Alcott's conception of the true teacher (LXXX)—that he
defends his pupils against his own personal influence, that
he inspires self-trust, that he will have no disciples, that
his life and teachings are but studies for yet nobler ideals.
In these sayings, and in the "Days from a Diary," which
followed the "Orphic Sayings," Alcott revealed, too, the
sweeter aspects of his character as it mellowed beneath the
surface of his trials and apparent worldly defeat—mellowed
and gathered strength for defeat still to come. As he planted
his seeds and worked among his currants and strawberries
on a May day, how genial the air and the sun! How dignified and dignifying was labor! Once more his self-respect
was whole and healthful, and all men, apostate though they
were, awarded sincere approval. Labor, after all, was sweet,

exalting and humanizing the soul. The upright man would not find it impossible, as he toiled in the field to earn his bread, to hold fast his integrity amidst all reverses. Though he might by his principles be exiled from the world, a solitary in his age, he could yet ripen for God. Over the plow, the spade, the sickle, man might discourse sublimely with divinity, marrying the soul and the soil by rites of labor. At night, there was the pillow to be sought with a weariness that made sleep grateful and refreshing.

Such were the reflections on thought and conduct which distinguished Alcott's contributions to the *Dial*.[2] But though this new journal now offered him an outlet for his views, and though he was finding a novel happiness in his village labors, Alcott's condition was not, in Emerson's judgment, what befitted him. This was not the pure success which, a year or two ago, Emerson had thought his friend needed. A touch of fame—the notice and approbation of those whose opinion mattered—this was what was wanting to Alcott. If only he might have the full pleasure of the joy in his genius expressed by his English friends—James Greaves and others—Alcott would yet have opportunity to expand his powers and to experience the notice rightfully his.

And so it was that Emerson conceived the plan of sending his friend to England. From England, several years back, after the Temple School had broken up, Alcott had received from James Pierrepont Greaves a friendly letter of inquiry concerning his educational methods. Greaves, who had been a reader of Boehme and a personal friend of Pestalozzi, as well as a teacher, had heard of the *Record of a School*. Later he wrote again for copies of the *Record* and of the *Conversations on the Gospels*. In Greaves's circle of English friends was John A. Heraud, editor of the *New Monthly Magazine,* which had printed a favorable review of Emerson's anonymously published *Nature,* and had mistakenly attributed the book to Alcott. Heraud had written, too, and had sent copies of his magazine. As a cap to these honors, Alcott learned that Greaves and his friends had established at Ham, Surrey, an infant school modeled after Alcott's own theories, and had named it the Alcott House School! That Alcott might enjoy this admiration to the full and draw new resources from it, Emerson volunteered to solicit from his acquaintances the funds necessary for a six-months journey to England. He assured Alcott that he could obtain $500, or more if necessary. Most of the money, actually, came out of Emerson's own pocket. Alcott sailed for England on the *Rosalind* on May 8, 1842, and did not return until October 20 of that year.

II

It was, for Emerson, a natural time for stocktaking of his relations with his friend, whom he had now known for seven years. They had been eventful years, for during them thoughts had come fast and full of excitement. There had been the pleasure of producing his first publications— *Nature,* in the thinking and writing of which Alcott had been such a sympathetic stimulus; *The American Scholar* and the Divinity School *Address,* which had created such a stir in Cambridge and Boston, a stir that the friends had talked about so many times; and now, recently, his first volume of *Essays.* As an author Emerson was acquiring a reputation that was reaching beyond the bounds of his native New England, and gradually his lecture engagements carried him farther and farther from home. In these years, too, as his thoughts crystallized into expression, the flush of enthusiasm and expectancy which had colored the horizon of his friendship became somewhat subdued. He grew more and more aware of his powers—and of his limitations, as well as those of his friend.

As for his opinion of Alcott, Emerson had already confessed to himself that neither Alcott nor any other friend—not even Elizabeth Hoar—could surprise him, could exalt him. Was it his own coldness or hardness that was to blame? But Alcott in his withdrawals from some of the minor irritations of the world he had long regarded as a modern stylite. And when Alcott wished to say that he could judge people by the ease with which he could offend them, Emerson believed he saw how puny and limitary were such egotisms. He wearied of them even though they belonged to so vast a spirit. It seemed to him sometimes, too, that his friend sought consciously to influence his thought, instead of being content with a free exchange of ideas. At such times the best he could do was to conclude that Alcott was a tedious archangel.

Now as he sat down in his study one day to write to Carlyle to announce Alcott's visit to England, he thought back over those seven years. His letter to Carlyle finished, he brought out his diary and tried to record there his current impressions of the friend whom he hoped to benefit by sending him to new and friendly surroundings.

Years later, when both were old men, Alcott, on his way to the post office one morning, met Emerson coming from his picket gate beneath the buckeye trees, and the two walked to the village together. Though Emerson's memory no longer served him well, his mind dwelt upon the past rather than the future. Their common history came to his mind this morning, and he revealed that he intended to write his friend's biography, if Alcott should withdraw first. In the pages of his diary, he said, he had all of Alcott's good things to show, and the world should yet know of his excellences.

But Emerson was not to outlive his friend, and his writing days were then really already over, as he himself

was sometimes aware. The notebook which he had marked
"A. B. A.," and in which he had written some notes and
indexed his journal references to Alcott, he never used.[3]
The friendly, justifying biography remained an old man's
dream.

Now, however, in 1842, his finished letter to Carlyle
beside him there in his study, his memory flooded with
the lively recollections of seven years, he was only at the
beginning of his maturity, his mind firm and focused only
on what he regarded as the honest realities of the present.
In the intimacy of his diary he, like Alcott, could be clear
and forthright when he chose, and this spring day was a
day for clarity and directness.[4]

III

It was plain, first of all, that Alcott was a man of ideas, a
man of faith. For all conventions, as such, one could expect
from him only contempt. It was true that his social nature
and his taste for beauty and magnificence sometimes betrayed him into tolerance and indulgence of men and magnificence; but on the whole he could be relied upon to judge
laws or practices by their essential wisdom or folly.

In nothing so much did he delight as in speculation,
and for this end was equipped with a remarkable vocabu-
lary. Nowhere was there a better converser than he. Yet
this gift of expression was limited solely to his speech, for
from the perusal of his writing one derived less pleasure than
pain. The newspaper in its rude humor spoke an element
of truth when it said that the "Orphic Sayings" resembled
a train of fifteen railroad cars with one passenger. And so
great was his delight in talking that he would willingly talk
all day, and most of the night, and then on and on for endless days. If one drew him out to walk in the woods or
fields, he would stop at the first fence and propose either to

sit down or to return. He seemed to think that life existed for talking, and judged literature good or bad as it suggested conversation, its highest form. Nevertheless, he always planted himself so swiftly and naturally on the moral sentiment that one could scarcely complain.

It was speculation that Alcott loved, not action. When the conversation was at an end, all was at an end. Tomorrow there was only more discourse, and not the celestial life to which his words would seem to have pledged him. Furthermore, he never remembered. He was an air plant, which put out no roots, but could readily and without ill results be transported anywhere. He was always quite ready to abandon his present ways to put into practice any new dream that bubbled up in the effervescence of discourse. He never affirmed anything one day because he had affirmed it before. And these traits stood in the way of action, though even by nature he seemed to have no vocation to labor, no talent for household uses. In spite of the fact that he preached labor for a time, and even made some efforts to practice it, he gave the impression that it depressed his spirits and was a cruel waste of his time.

Sometimes the imprudence of his behavior and the enormity of his expressions shocked people of decorum; still, he had a serene and lofty aspect and deportment in the street and in the house, a noble bearing, and simple but graceful and majestic manners. True enough, he had a great sense of his own worth, offset, however, by a strong love of men, so that in spite of his long poverty, he had been as generous and hospitable, as munificent in his own way, as the richest merchant in Boston. His love of men led him, too, to an insatiable curiosity concerning all who were distinguished either by intellect or by character; and anyone who conversed with him was soon sensible that here was a man for a public crisis, for any situation demanding great courage, great sacrifice, self-immolation.

This commanding love of speculation was accompanied by a grand dream to realize a reform in the life of man. This was the steadily returning, the monotonous topic of years of conversation. He was enticed by this interest to reformers of all shades and peculiarities, who soon disappointed him by their coarseness and ignorance, yet who, during their periods of influence, drew him into coldness and quarrels with the refined and conservative scholars. So he spent his days in these oscillations, back and forth, between the scholars and the reformers—a tedious and dispiriting spectacle.

His greatest vice was a certain brooding on the private thought which produced a monotony in his conversation and an egotism in his character. He could find no pleasure in the variety of external facts so necessary to the health of most minds, but must always come back to himself, so that his constant reflection seemed to be—*Alcott in reference to the world of today.* Unhappily, though he saw the law of man truer and farther than anyone ever did, his conversation never lost sight of his own personality. The poet, rapt into future times or into deeps of nature admired for themselves, lost in their law, cheered one with a lively charm; but this noble genius, Alcott, discredited genius. One could not wish any more such persons to exist.

IV

When Emerson was thus criticizing his friend, he was, for all his forthrightness, nevertheless moving in a labyrinth of criticism through which his own way may not yet have been clear. Perhaps the most hypercritical portions of his remarks were aimed at himself quite as much as at Alcott. It is true that his comment on the "Orphic Sayings"—their

ample space and small cargo—applied rather to manner
than to content; he discovered no fault with their thoughts,
which were largely his own. But when he found in Alcott
an undue love of speculation, he was apparently reversing
his own earlier judgment that his friend should leave an
unprofitable field of action for a life of contemplation. It
was Alcott, in the first years of their acquaintance, who had
urged action! It was Emerson who, in *The American
Scholar,* was quoting Alcott on the virtues of action! Curiously enough, now, in the past, and in years to come, it was
a question hard for both to settle. Just what was the proper
blend of action and of speculation? As for Alcott not
remembering, there, in print in the *Essays,* were Emerson's
own fine words about a foolish consistency and the *whim*
written on the lintels of his doorpost. For Alcott's monotonous topic of reform, Emerson had, in these years, however, a steady suspicion. Society, he had written, never
advances. Though it undergoes changes, there is no amelioration. It was later that both friends met on the common
ground of the reform of slavery, and later that Emerson
came to believe that the destiny of organized nature is
amelioration, and that it is for man to tame the chaos. And
when Emerson complained that Alcott's constant reflection
was the world in reference to himself, had he forgotten that
he himself had said that the scholar, in going down into the
secrets of his own mind, has descended into the secrets of
all minds?

Had he forgotten these things, or was he awakening
to the limitations of his own thought, testing it, perhaps,
in the light of an experience which, though apparently invalid and vain from the viewpoint of faith, yet had its claims
in the eyes of the world? For Emerson the years ahead were
restless ones, full of self-examination, criticism of others,
a weighing of philosophies, his own included. He was still

capable of the ecstasy of "The Over-Soul," but such rhapso-
dies suffered their periods of interruption. Before him, indeed, lay maturity, the long level years.

v

In the meanwhile, however, while Alcott was beyond
the sea, there were for Emerson new experiences in friendship. For one, there was his growing acquaintance with
Ellery Channing, the young poet whose ambition he was
trying to stir. Ellery loved to walk, and when he came out
from Cambridge, the two explored the Concord fields together. Ellery had an observant eye, and in a degree filled
the vacancy left long ago by the death of Charles. The
sunset, he said, makes us think of our lack of men equal
to it, though at last who can say what we seem to know
of nature? How well known to us are certain winds, certain lights, certain aspects of the soil and the grove. Yet
what words can begin to convey what these mean? It is all
unutterable. But Ellery, in spite of these fine glances and
a poetry like an exquisite nerve communicating by thrills,
was a very imperfect artist, and, unfortunately, now seemed
unequal to finish anything. He was as satisfied with his
poor as with his good—would, in fact, have it all pass for
good. Emerson found him disappointing—disappointing
because he would not bestir himself to do his best, would
not or could not acquit himself in accomplishments which
the world might justly expect. He was, however, very good
company, with his taste, and his cool, hard, sensible behavior, yet with the capacity of melting to emotion, or of
wakening to the most genial mirth.[5]

More interesting than Ellery just now was Hawthorne,
who had only recently settled in the Old Manse. He was
the more welcome because he and his newly married wife
were friends of Elizabeth Hoar, who had enticed them to

Concord after Hawthorne had left Brook Farm. Emerson
had visited the newlyweds at the Manse, his own ancestral
home, where Hawthorne was now occupying the study beneath the old willow which had brushed the windows when
Nature was taking form. Emerson, too, had shown Hawthorne his wood-paths to Walden Pond. Then, one fine
day late in September, as a kind of dedication of their
friendship, the two set forth on a walk to Harvard village,
where Emerson's father had had his first pastorate, before
Emerson was born. The day was full of sunshine, and it
was a luxury to walk in the midst of all this warm and
colored light. They took a westward course, along the
Assabet, the north branch of the Concord, toward the
Damon mills, now standing still, the workers' houses empty.
But the little Assabet was still active, falling over the rocks
into silver, and expanding above into a tranquil lake. Almost
reluctantly they turned away to take the road to Stow,
though new sights soon engaged their interests. A thorn-
bush with red berries, wild apple trees whose fruit hung
like pendants, and grapevines trailing the stone walls, were
the decorations of their path. They looked wistfully back
at some fringed gentians which they longed to pick.

Though they scarcely encountered man or boy on the
road, nor saw any in the fields, the outlines of the landscape
were so gentle that it seemed they were in a very cultivated country and that elegant people must be living over
yonder hills. Several times they appeared to be at the
entrance of lordly parks, though nothing in the farms or
houses really made the promise good. They reflected that in
Europe such land would be full of men of the best stock,
of the best culture, whose pride it would be to fill these
establishments with every convenience and ornament. Here,
where the best minds, at sixteen or twenty years, were sent
to New York or Boston, the land was tilled by an inferior

class of people; hence there remained nothing but these shiftless, poverty-struck pig farms. It was disappointing.

There were no incidents in their walk, but they needed none, for they were in excellent spirits, and there was much conversation. Both were old collectors who had never had opportunity before to show each other their cabinets; so they could have filled much longer days. They entertained themselves, however, with fancied incidents. Suppose some vagary of their brain took them into these "huts where poor men lie," to use Wordsworth's words. Suppose they asked dinner or a night's lodging. Might it not be easy to break into some mesh of domestic romance, learn so much pathetic private history, perhaps see a blush mantle on the cheeks of some young girl when the mail stage came or did not come, or even get entangled themselves in some thread of gold or grey? But nothing of the kind happened. There they were, two sober men who kept on the outside of the land and did not so much as ask for a glass of milk at a farmhouse door. Even when they stopped at a tavern, there was no event. In an earlier day they might have shared the joke and the politics of the teamster and the farmers on the road. But now the temperance society had emptied the barroom. It was a cold and uninteresting place. Hawthorne tried to smoke a cigar there, but soon was out on the piazza.

They reached Stow after noon, dined, and continued on their way towards Harvard village. The last miles of their journey they rode in a wagon, a friendly, fatherly man, who knew Emerson's name and Emerson's father's name and history, having asked them to ride. The old gentleman insisted on doing the honors of his town—installed them at the tavern, introduced them to his friends, and demanded the landlord's best attention to their wants. It was a triumphal entry, and a welcome end to a journey of twenty miles.

Somewhat after six next morning they began their walk

for the Shaker village, three and a half miles distant. There
they ate breakfast and examined the farm, the barn, the
orchard, the vineyard—the last containing, Emerson observed, two beautiful arcades of grapes, both white and Isa-
bella, full of fruit. Some of the brethren they engaged in
conversation, not altogether successfully because Emerson
was crippled this morning by a barking cold, and Hawthorne was inclined to play Jove more than Mercurius. But
between them they learned something about the Society,
Emerson taking pleasure in being downright with the downright and not hesitating to ask a question when he had a
question in mind. They were an interesting group, he
thought, particularly so since their experiment of socialism
fell in with the temper of the times. He remembered with
some amusement, however, a spirit-level which he had
found on a window seat in one of the houses. At first he
had thought it a very good emblem for the Society; but
then he had discovered that neither the table nor the shelf
nor the window seat were plumb!

From the Shaker village the friends walked homeward
through Littleton and Acton, the countryside still in the
same redundance of splendor. It was like a day in July, and
they sauntered leisurely. Somewhat, as they walked, they
had to say about the Shakers—how people came and proved
themselves as members, remaining or departing, as the
Spirit made manifest, alike to themselves or to the Society;
how no man should join them for a living, none turned
away because he was poor or bedridden, but only for not
being of them. They talked, too, of Landor and of Scott.
Like other poets, Landor had not been happy in love, though
he had written admirable sentences on the passion. Perhaps, said Hawthorne, disappointment taught the poets to
write well. Both agreed, speculatively, that a sentence of
Landor's was worth a divorce! When they spoke of Scott,

they agreed, too, that there is some greatness in defying posterity and writing for the hour, and so being a harper. Was it not true, also, that piety, like chivalry, has no stationary exemplar, but is evanescent and receding like a rainbow? You cannot find any specimen of a religious man now in your society; you hear the fame of one; you go far and find him; and he begins, "I had a friend in my youth." Yet it seems as if nothing would make such good picture in national sketches as genuine Connecticut, if you could lay your hand on it.

The nineteen miles of their second day were finished before four in the afternoon. In his diary Emerson remarked that there is something very agreeable in fatigue. The days of September are so rich, it seemed to him, that it is natural to walk to the end of one's strength, and then fall prostrate, saturated with the fine floods, and say, Now, Lord, let thy servant depart. Hawthorne remembered the journey because it was the first time in his life that he had ever come home, for he had never before had a home. He recollected nothing so well as the fringed gentians by the roadside.[6]

VI

Alcott, in England, was the cynosure in a circle of adulating friends. He was introduced to many men of literary and philosophic distinction, and his arrival, as Emerson observed in the *Dial*, was made the occasion of meetings for public conversation on the great ethical questions of the day. In a quiet nook of Old England he was beholding the first substantial admission of his claim to be considered the exponent of what his admirers regarded as a divinely inspired idea—his theory of infant instruction. Greaves, who had corresponded with Alcott in America, and who had been chiefly responsible for the establishment of the Alcott House School, had unfortunately died shortly before Alcott's arrival in England. But Alcott met H. G. Wright, who was now head of the school, and for him felt the greatest respect. Wright had more genius for teaching, Alcott thought, than any person he had ever seen—impersonated and realized better his own idea of an education. Alcott also met Charles Lane, who, with Wright, edited the *Healthian,* and, like Wright, contributed to almost every reform journal in the kingdom. These, with others who had been interested in the Alcott House School, now that Greaves was dead, looked to Alcott for inspiration. It was, for Alcott, an intoxicating experience. He had not been in England more than a month before he conceived the plan of bringing some of his friends to America—here to establish a New Eden, an ideal community in which all the cherished reforms might be instituted. It seemed that his hour had come at last.[7]

At home in Concord, Emerson, editing the *Dial,* was kept supplied with news and manuscripts from Alcott and his English friends. Editorially he commented on these communications, assuring his readers that these papers spoke to the conscience. But he could not refrain from saying that they likewise had many sins to answer for—an abundance of superficiality, of pedantry, of inflation, of lack of thought. It seemed to him as if these sanguine schemers rushed to the press with every notion that danced before their brain. He could, after a fashion, tolerate the views even of the most extreme of Alcott's friends, but he complained humorously that there ought to be a respect, if not for English church and state, at least for English grammar! To his friends in New England he wrote gayly that when Alcott arrived with his captive Englishmen they might expect the faint radicalism of the *Dial* to become a downright sans-culottism. At his own house, when Lidian was informed that Alcott was bringing the English reformers to Concord, and when she thereupon proclaimed that they should not be permitted in their good village, he teased his wife by saying that she would yet entreat them to come to her, though in vain. In more serious moments he reflected that men are delicate ware to bring across the sea, more delicate than Sèvres porcelain and glass, or than tropical fruit, for the least nonreception of them in the thought and heart of those to whom they come makes cruelty, futility, and confusion.

When, however, Alcott arrived with his English friends, Emerson did what he could to welcome them to Concord. The travelers brought with them a thousand volumes, chiefly mystical and philosophical books, which Emerson saw safely through the customhouse in Boston. To his brother William he wrote that thereafter Concord would scarcely need the moon any longer o' nights! Later, one November afternoon, he invited Alcott, Wright, and Lane to his home, to unfold their idea of a true social institution, the plan for the New Eden. George Ripley and all Brook Farm came in strength to hear the conversation, as did Hawthorne and others. But for the most part, Emerson found it almost impossible to isolate his old friend or the newcomers for an exchange of reasonable words. Lane, who seemed to be a man of fine powers and elevated character, he tried to detach and bring to his house, as a sort of cooling furnace, or a place where he might be partially corrupted and fitted for the grosser realities of Yankee land. But Lane remained only a day or two, and then fled to join Wright and Alcott at the latter's cottage. There the three held perpetual parliament, all day and all night, creating new solar systems, as Emerson wrote in a sprightly letter to Margaret Fuller, and shaping the prospective education in the nebulae.

On the whole, the conversations and the grand schemes of the triumvirate were disappointing and wearisome to

Emerson. At first, when he had examined the library which they had brought from England, and when he had realized what a rich collection it really was, and what a remarkable fact in American literary history, he had thought of his old plan of an ideal university, taught by the best of teachers in the land and open to all who had a love of truth. None of these men, alas, were gifted as leaders. They were admirable instruments for a master's hand, if some instituting Pythagoras, some marshaling Mirabeau, some royal Alfred were at hand. Such a man could not have better professors than Alcott and Lane and Wright. All these, however, were too desultory, ignorant, imperfect, and whimsical to be trusted for any progress—excellent springs, worthless regulators. As for Alcott particularly, he was a singular person, a natural Levite, a priest forever after the order of Melchizedek, whom all good persons would readily combine to maintain as a priest to live in his own cottage—literary, spiritual, and choosing his own methods of teaching and action. But for a founder of a family or an institution, Emerson concluded that he would as soon exert himself to collect money for a madman.[8]

With the plans for the New Eden, the new doctrines of social life, Emerson was almost wholly out of sympathy. The remark of the three reformers that business was an evil and that they had done with it, he confessed made him sick. Here was the dear, grand Alcott who would dig in a field for a day, charge a dollar, and yet not call it a business transaction. We might very well and honestly have theoretical and practical objections to money. If such objections were fatal to the use of money and barter, we should disuse them; if less grave than the inconvenience of abolishing traffic, we should not pretend to have done with it, whilst we eat and drink and wear and breathe it. The folly of his friends in their attitude toward money seemed all the more apparent to Emerson because, in their dreams of the ideal community, they began with the assumption that they should be given a farm—a farm of a hundred acres, in excellent condition, with good buildings, a good orchard, and grounds which admitted of being laid out with great beauty. Such a beginning, it seemed to Emerson, argued nothing. Many innocent young people would find it relatively easy to prosper and to retain their innocency under such circumstances. But who would be instructed and strengthened by tranquillity obtained in such an easy fashion? How insignificant and meaningless such a procedure! It would be quite another matter if, unaided, in the midst of poverty, toil, and business, they should extricate themselves from these hindrances, and build on their land a house of peace and benefit, good customs, and free thoughts. A fatal fault of the schemers, he thought, was that they assumed that their whole doctrine was spiritual, whereas they always ended with saying, Give us land and money.

Could they not die? or succeed, or help themselves, or draw others? or be disposed of, in any manner that might take them from his horizon—these men who were too great to be neglected, and not great enough to be of any aid or comfort to this great craving humanity? He evaded their presence by spending much of the winter from home. It was a great joy to get away from such persons and to live again under the dominion of the multiplication table. Could they but once understand that he loved to know that they existed, that he wished them Godspeed, yet out of the poverty of his life and thought had no word of welcome for them when they came to see him, and that he could well consent to their living in another town, from any claim on them that he felt, it would be a great satisfaction.

Fortunately for Emerson's peace of mind, there were for him amusing circumstances in the conduct of his old friend

and the Englishmen. At the Alcott cottage, the proving
ground of the prospective New Eden, there were going
forward manifold experiments in diet based on principles
of health and social conduct. Rice they would not eat
because it came from an East where serfdom still prevailed;
nor molasses, because it was made by the labor of slaves.
Shoes of leather were objectionable because their making
involved the killing of animals; woolen clothing robbed
sheep of their wool. Yet these hypersensitive abstainers had
no scruples in accepting gold coins with which to buy
wheat and rye, maple sugar or an oaken chest, though such
coins were, it seemed to Emerson, as much as anything else,
horsehide and sheepskin, rice and molasses! Moreover,
though he himself had literally run away from the seemingly endless discourse at the Alcott cottage, he had found
amusement in it too—once he was safely out of range. He
was entertained by the story of the little Alcott girl who
had been sent to report whether the reformer-philosophers
had ended their talk long enough to perform some necessary
household task, and who had returned with the unhappy
answer, "Mamma, they have begun again!"

Nevertheless, when, late in May, preparations were
actually completed for the departure to the New Eden,
Emerson was full of regrets. He was sad at heart that these
divine lotus eaters could not have from him that love and
service to which they seemed, by their aims and the com-
plexion of their minds, as well as by their unpopularity, to
have rich claims. Especially did it seem to him that he had
treated Charles Lane with the worst inhospitality. Never
had he really received that man to him, though he thought
of Lane as a pure, superior, mystical, intellectual, and
gentle soul—free and youthful in character, too. It was
strange that Lane had always treated him with such marked
forbearance—Lane, who was so formidable, such a fighter

in the ring. Though Lane had stayed so long in his neighborhood, he had remained an alien. The difficulty was,
Emerson recognized, that Lane's nature did not invite his
own, but always froze him. Lane was a born warrior, the
most expert swordsman Emerson had ever seen, and good
when the trumpet sounded. He was metallic in character,
not vegetable enough. He had no eye for nature, and his
hands, alas, were as far from his head as Alcott's own!

At the bottom of Emerson's skepticism of the venture
in the New Eden was his conviction that this hegira was
not a winging toward the ideal, but a simple flight from
reality. In his diary he represented the situation and his
own reactions by a story from his reading in the Chinese
Four Books. It was a story of Chang Tsoo and Kee Neih,
who had retired from the state to the fields, because society
seemed to them full of wrong and misrule. They were impatient with Confucius, who elected to remain in the world.
"Ah," sighed Confucius, "I cannot associate with birds and
beasts. If I follow not man, whom shall I follow?" If
the world were in possession of right principles, he should
not seek to stay and change it. Under the circumstances, he
chose to cast his lot with the world.

VII

The truth was that Emerson had made up his mind
about "union," or "association," or "community" long before his friend Alcott had proposed his particular plans for
associative living. Though he tentatively considered the
possibility of joining his forces with those of George Ripley
when Ripley proposed the project which became Brook
Farm, Emerson never wholly favored the idea. From the
very first he had thought that Ripley's plan of a community
in the country, where each member would participate in the
manual labor, implied an unnecessary emphasis on one

kind of work. He himself had some theories of self-help, and he was not averse to manual labor. Though he felt that he had no aptitude with his hands, he took a kind of pleasure in drudging about his house and acres, carrying rails into the shed under his barn or digging parsnips in the garden with a dung-fork. On winter mornings, he enjoyed carrying armfuls of wood to his study from the great wood-pile in the yard near the barn. Such tasks gave him exercise and were welcome interruptions in a sedentary life. But was it not pedantry to insist that every man should be a farmer as much as that he should be a lexicographer? If the doctrine of universal labor should find a man in the midst of books, whose use he understood, and whose use other men wished to learn of him, should he cast away his skill and usefulness to go bungle with hoe and harrow, with cows and swine which he did not understand? Should he not rather farm his books well and lose no hour of beneficent activity in the place where he found himself? And was it not the experience of all who did heavy labor that they had no thoughts?

There were, however, even more serious objections. When George Ripley and Sophia, his wife, and Margaret Fuller and Alcott had come to his home one October day to discuss the new social plans, Emerson had decided that this scheme was arithmetic and comfort, a hint borrowed from luxurious hotels, a rage in our poverty and politics to live rich and gentlemanlike, an anchor to leeward against change of weather, a prudent forecast on the probable issue of the great questions of pauperism and poverty. This scheme, indeed, was fundamentally at odds with his own theory of self-help. Take away from a man the feeling that he must depend on himself, give him the least hint that he had good friends and backers there in reserve to help him, and would he not instantly relax his diligence? In such an experiment it might be expected that a few, like the Ripleys, perhaps, would identify themselves with the community, a few noble victims who would act and suffer with temper and proportion.   The others would be experimenters who would stay if the community throve, but who would be always ready to retire in the presence of adversity; that is, the larger part would be slight adventurers who would shirk work.   Furthermore, granting the advisability or the practicability of the scheme, uncertain as these matters might be, there remained Emerson's doubts about Ripley.   Amiable and accomplished as Ripley was, Emerson was unable to find in him the enterprise which Ripley wished to take in hand.   It was all theory with Ripley, not an essential part of the man.   He was adopting the reform by the ear and by the understanding from the books he had been reading. His action was tentative, a part of the city carried out into the fields, and was the city still, and no new fact, and could not inspire Emerson's enthusiasm.   Ripley was, in short, not the man to lead such an undertaking.

Convincing as these objections were to Emerson, there were yet others that probed still greater depths of his thought and temperament.   Ever since he had read Goethe's *Wilhelm Meister,* years ago, it had been a first principle with him, when he considered reform, to think of the dross in his own bosom.   Now he reflected that he had not yet conquered his own house. It irked and repented him. Should he raise the siege of a hencoop, and march baffled away to a pretended siege of Babylon?   It seemed to him that to do so were to dodge the problem he was set to solve, and to hide his impotency in the thick of a crowd.   Yes, a renovation of institutions and a destruction of drudgery there should be, but not in the way of the reformers—Ripley, or Fourier, or Owen, or Alcott—and not as these thought, but only as union is combined with isolation: silent union, actual separateness; ideal union, actual independence. Each man being the universe, if he attempt to join himself to others, he is instantly jostled, crowded, cramped, halved, quartered, or on all sides diminished of his proportion, and, the stricter the union, the less and more pitiful he is. But let him go alone, he will go up and down doing the works of a true member, and, to the astonishment of all, the whole work will be done with concert, though no man spoke; government will be adamantine without any governor. Let every man shovel out his own snow, and the whole city will be passable. The whole problem for Emerson resolved itself into this: If he joined Ripley's community he would be denying his most basic convictions and the instinct which spoke from them—that a man is a counterpoise to a city, that a man is stronger than a city, and that his solitude is more prevalent and beneficent than the concert of crowds. Ultimately, the Divine Spirit detaches.[9] The essence of worship (the source from which all good thought springs and to which it returns) is as Plotinus said—a flight of the alone to the Alone.

Actually, therefore, Emerson was not for long beset by speculative doubts over the question of joining with Ripley. To Lidian, who had been in Boston a week or more early in November, he wrote a bantering letter urging her to hasten home to prevent her dangerous husband from selling his property and joining the community, or from inviting a whole troop of new tenants into his own house. To Margaret Fuller he wrote more seriously, expressing what alone really disturbed him—that the least weight should hang upon his decision, that his friends should place such importance on his choice, as if the fate of the project rested with him. His letter of refusal to Ripley was simple and clear: he did not think the community good for him or he for it. The reforms which he favored could as well begin at home and would not be advantaged by the sale of his house and the removal of his family. He would regard the community with lively sympathy and with a sort of gratitude, glad that it should be, and hopeful that it might aid others.

The making of these choices settled for Emerson the question of community. He was therefore not disposed to change his mind when Alcott and his friends laid before him the more extreme designs for living in the New Eden.

VIII

It was a sharp and cold afternoon early in June when Lane and the Alcotts arrived at the farm which was to be the scene of their new experiment in associative living. The place was not of Alcott's choosing. Alcott had preferred the cliffs overlooking the Sudbury River where it narrowed below Fairhaven Bay. One May afternoon he and Lane had walked from Concord along the river to this spot, high above the stream where it passed by a dark clump of trees, and where nature charmed the eye with her distinct and perfect painting. Here, as they sauntered through the woodland or paused to talk in the young orchard, Alcott's head had been full of poetic dreams of a cottage, and gardens, and fields. It was a scene loved by Emerson and Thoreau, too. But it was Lane's money which was to make their scheme possible, and so Alcott had to yield the point. Lane had chosen the Wyman farm, about fourteen miles from Concord, and some two miles from the village of Harvard. They had decided to call their new home Fruitlands, because, eventually, fruit was to be their chief article of food.

When all was said and done, however, Alcott was not displeased with Lane's choice. For picturesque beauty of landscape, the spot had few rivals near Concord. It lay some distance from a public road, with not another house to break the view, and breathed quiet and tranquillity. From the highest part, the friends agreed, the prospect was sublime. A semicircle of undulating mountains stretched from south to west, Wachusett and Monadnoc conspicuous in the distance, the whole scene disposed in green hills and valleys, in fields and woods. The house itself stood on the slope of a slowly descending strip of land, with a grove of trees and Still River beyond, and the Shaker village across the stream and still farther away. There were clusters of nut trees, maples, and pines, and from the granite hills above broke several springs of delicious water—none better, they thought, in Massachusetts. They might have done much worse than choose these ninety acres, even as an investment, as Lane surmised, or for fertility and ease of cultivation, as Alcott believed.

The old red farmhouse, however, was dilapidated and the worse for wear, ill-placed and unsightly, as well as inconvenient. It was crowded, too, for the utopians consisted now, not only of the Alcotts and their four daughters, and of Lane and his young son, but of several others, also, a varying number, Wright having decided that the dietary rules were too strict for him, and others coming and going for various reasons. The children were therefore obliged for a while to sleep in the attic, though they did not mind—enjoyed, rather, on warm summer nights, the sound of the rain on the roof.

The men were too busy during the day to be concerned with such inconveniences. Only a small part of the farm had been put to crops when the purchase was made, and consequently there was much to do. Alcott worked steadily at the plow, Lane marveling at the straightness of his furrow. They planted corn and potatoes, and sowed rye and oats, barley and buckwheat, peas and beans, melons and squashes, for, since they had renounced the eating of flesh, fruits and grains and vegetables were to be their only food, and they wished to be as nearly as possible self-subsisting. They had wanted to forego animal labor; but the lateness of their beginnings had compelled a compromise with necessity, and so they had put the oxen to the yoke. As they worked in their fields, they were a strange sight to their curious neighbors, for all, men and women and children alike, wore trousers and tunics and broad-brimmed hats—all of brown linen. They believed in simplicity of clothing, and the wearing of cotton or wool was for them forbidden.

Sometimes, as they rested from their planting and other labors, Alcott and Lane walked proudly about their estate, consoling themselves with the thought that the present actualities would soon yield to manifold better things. The poor accommodations of the old house need not long be endured. There, in the nearer copse, their new cottages would stand. It would be no great task to lead water to every house from the springs on the upper hill. Gardens would displace the meadows on the south where the cattle now grazed. Some day there would be bounteous orchards, and Fruitlands would justify its name. A little clearing of their brook, and the river would be accessible by their boat. Only a Thoreau was needed to point out the classic beauty of their woodland acres. It eased their tired bodies thus to look around their farm, seeing what was growing, learning the shape of their fields, pondering the capabilities of the land.

Nor was every day spent in the fields. For the children there was always an occasional leisure hour, and now and then an idyllic day for all. Sometimes the children ran on the high hill, breasting the wind or playing fairies, and pretending that they were flying in the air. Sometimes there were walks in the woods in which all joined, children and grownups, too. There the girls made for their parents wreaths of oak leaves decorated with flowers, and thus classically adorned mother and father and the rest marched home. On Elizabeth's birthday, late in June, the whole group went to the woods, where presents were hung on a little pine tree. Lane played his violin, and they all sang. Alcott read a birthday ode that he had written, and asked each to give an emblematic flower. Lane gave a piece of moss, for humility. (Elizabeth was eight.) Sometimes, later in the year, there were expeditions for blueberries, or after dark, they had lamps in the barn and all joined in the fun of husking corn. On winter days Mrs. Alcott read to the girls as they sewed, or Alcott entertained the whole family with their beloved *Pilgrim's Progress*. It was incidents such as these which they permitted themselves to recall in after years, when not all memories of Fruitlands would have been pleasant ones.[10]

IX

Visitors came now and then. In mid-June Emerson had been invited. He came, with Ellery Channing, to spend the Fourth of July, but he had not been convinced that all was going as well as Alcott and Lane wished him to believe.[11] Their appearance, their talk, privately amused him. They reminded him of nothing so much as The Three at Felix's Wonderful Institution. Though the sun and the evening sky did not look calmer than they, he would not prejudge them successful; he would see them in December. A month later Ellery had walked the fourteen miles from Concord to Harvard, and upon his return had spoken to Emerson of his visit. From what Ellery said, Emerson inferred that the society at Fruitlands would have no great stability. Alcott, it seemed, was sadly anticipating the time when he should be forsaken of all. Some of the others could not sympathize with his asceticism. Lane was very much engaged with the Shakers across Still River. And Alcott was not well.

Sometimes Lane and Alcott left their labors for journeys to Boston or Concord or Brook Farm. Late in July they had stopped in Concord a few moments on their way to Boston, though they had said nothing of their errand, and Emerson had not liked to ask. Their real destination was Roxbury, where they spent the evening at Brook Farm, shocked at the miserably joyous, frivolous manner in which these eighty or ninety people were playing away their youth. Most of the adults were there, they concluded, only for a good time. What could be expected of the education at Brook Farm when there was so much shallow emphasis on the languages? They were repulsed by the prominent position which Ripley gave to animals—the numerous horses and cows and oxen and pigs—and to commerce with Boston. In the whole community there were not above four or five who were truly progressive beings, among whom anything deeper than ordinary could be found. The society at Roxbury was merely one of taste—nothing deeper.

In September, Lane had spent two days in Concord with Emerson. He had come—as was the custom of the Fruit-landers now—dressed altogether in linen, with the exception of his shoes, which were lined with linen, and he wore no stockings. In spite of what Emerson had heard of some rift in the affairs at Fruitlands, Lane was full of methods of an improved life. His mind dwelt much on getting rid of animals. They were not an economy on a farm. Particularly was he concerned about the offensiveness of their slaughter and use as food. It was only a subterfuge to put off upon a second or third person the act of serving or of killing cattle. The act would be sure to come back on the offender in some shape or other, as in the brutality of the person one had brutalized. These objections Emerson recorded in his diary with some sympathy, for he himself had had his moments of revulsion. But there was, in his judgment, no use denying it up and down—the way of providence was a little rude. Race lived at the expense of race. That, indeed, was the condition upon which life was permitted; and so vegetarianism settled nothing. As for Lane, he came away from his visit with a sense of disappointment, too. Emerson, he assured himself, was quite stationary, quite off the railroad of progress. He was merely an elegant, kindly observer of all who passed onward, noting down their aspects while they remained in sight, and, of course, forgetting them as soon as they had arrived at a new station beyond his vision. In such worthy scribblers Lane had small faith. He hoped that there were others of more real and more solid virtue.

Late in the autumn Alcott came to see Emerson, though he felt estranged from his old Concord friend. At Fruitlands he had expressed his present impatience with what he regarded as Emerson's aloofness from participation in the reforms of the day. The whole world, he had said, was to Emerson only a lecture room—nothing more. And of this impatience Emerson was not unaware. He saw that while he and other men were content to deck the dullness of the months with here and there a fine action or hope, Alcott was satisfied with nothing less than weaving the whole in a new texture of truth and beauty. Here was Alcott, this magnificent dreamer, brooding, as ever, on the renewal of the social fabric after ideal law, heedless that he had been uniformly rejected by every class to whom he had addressed himself, and just as sanguine and vast as ever. Here he was, this wandering emperor, from year to

year making his round of visits from house to house of such
as did not exclude him, seeking a companion, tired of pupils.
It was very pathetic.

X

It was pathetic, perhaps even more so than Emerson
then conjectured, and much more so, certainly, than Alcott
would as yet confess. Not all was going well at Fruitlands,
as Emerson had foreseen. It is true that Alcott and Lane
shared many views which they hoped to realize at Fruitlands. Even before he had made his journey to England
and there met Lane, Alcott had believed that man has no
moral claim whatever to property, that use, not ownership,
constitutes his sole privilege. He was therefore in accord
with Lane when Lane solemnly made Fruitlands an offering to the Eternal Spirit, resigned his rights in the farm,
and deeded the land—in the absence of any other legal
means of dealing with that Spirit!—to Mrs. Alcott's brother
as trustee. They were in agreement, too, on the question
of trade and money, Alcott's views on which had so greatly
irritated Emerson. They would be self-subsisting as far as
possible, and such articles as they could not make they would
endeavor to obtain by friendly exchanges. On matters of
diet, on abstaining from flesh, on the use only of fruits
and vegetables and grains, and on refraining from any kind
of stimulating drinks—tea, or coffee, or liquors—they had
no differences. In their views on the employment of animals they were likewise in accord—in the wrongfulness of
subjugating them to labor; in the folly of serving them as
cook and chambermaid; in the belief that if animals were
disposed of, one fourth of the land then tilled would
suffice for human needs; in the repugnance at animal ma-
nures; and in the conviction that green-crop fertilizers were
superior. The march of science and the making of money

they were sure had only added to the degradation of man, and no good would come from a knowledge of how to double the crops of the earth. In these and in many other details their minds were at one. Even in regard to more abstract principles they agreed. Perhaps paradoxically for those who would build an isolated ideal community, they held in common the belief that the evils of life are not so much social, or political, as personal, and that only a personal reform can eradicate them. Both also were persuaded that being, in preference to doing, is the great aim, and that being comes to us rather by a resigned willingness than by a willful activity, which is a check to all divine growth. An active occupation in human improvements, unless inwardly well motivated, never attains to, but rather hinders, divine progress in man. It was an abstruse point. In its essence it represented nothing different from what Alcott had long believed or what was firm doctrine with Emerson, though sometimes, to Alcott's more skeptical friends, the principle seemed to excuse inactivity; but the emphasis was apparently no longer where Alcott had once placed it— on the conviction that no idea is complete until it is realized in an act, that old conviction which he and Emerson had once so enthusiastically shared in the first years of their friendship.[12]

In none of these beliefs were Alcott and Lane at odds. In none of these was there any need that the one struggle to persuade the other of his point of view. If, however, there was at the beginning of their relationship no essential conflict of opinion concerning one question, which, under the circumstances, was very important, there developed a difference that demanded a surrender or threatened a disruption. From the early days of his reading in Pestalozzi, Alcott had been peculiarly charmed by the beneficent possibilities of the motherly affections, the gentle and binding influence of

children, the joyous and elevating experiences evoked by
family life. In the first winter of his residence in Concord,
in the year which he then thought the least hopeful of his
life, he had yet copied into his diary a saying of Hierocles.
"A married life," Hierocles had said, "is beautiful. For
what other thing can be such an ornament to a family as
the association of husband and wife?" And Alcott had
agreed, for no other sentiment, indeed, had ever been more
characteristic of him or had given him more solace in his
adversity.

XI

Then, at Fruitlands, matters had taken a startling turn.
One of their associates for a short while had been Isaac
Hecker, a restless seeker whose doubts and asceticism led
him at last into monkish orders. One day late in July, he
and Alcott and Lane had gathered, as usual, after supper,
for an evening of conversation, and Alcott had asked Hecker
for his first impressions regarding the hindrances he had
noted since his arrival at Fruitlands. It was not the kind
of question that might draw assurances of amity, nor was
Hecker the kind of young man to avoid an unceremonious
answer. There were, he said, not enough fruit trees on the
farm; too much time was spent with literature and writing
for the success of the enterprise; Alcott himself was not
sufficiently frank, and, instead of co-operating with others,
insisted too much on his own aims; and Alcott's family
were preventing his immediate plans of reformation.

As for Alcott's reactions to these criticisms, the reference
to his family was apparently only one of the straws in the
wind, for in the next month he had permitted his signature
to accompany an article which Lane had written regarding
their common objectives in the associative life, an article
which gave guarded approval to an examination of the

virtues of the Shaker practices of celibacy and a separation of the sexes. This new relation of the sexes, Lane had written, had led to results more harmonic than was possible in the usual family arrangements. Perhaps the great secular success of the Shakers, their order, their cleanliness, their intelligence, their serenity, might be attributed to their denial of marriage and customary family life.

Early in December, Lane had been in Concord again to see Emerson, a visit which Emerson recounted to Margaret Fuller in a letter blending, as he loved to do in his intimate correspondence, seriousness and raillery. Lane had just been released from jail, where he had been placed for nonpayment of his taxes (perhaps on principle, like Alcott, earlier that year). But it was not for this that he was sad and indisposed. The trouble was that he and Alcott had now discovered that all these years they had been wrong in lauding, with Pestalozzi, the maternal instinct and the family. These, said Emerson, they now thought the very mischief! These they now regarded as selfish and opposing the success of a community based on universal love. Margaret should yet see how it would all turn out![13] In his diary, somewhat later, Emerson recorded his most recent impression of the Shakers for whom Lane had taken such a fancy. It was a less complimentary view than the one he had had on that memorable holiday, now more than a year ago, when he had walked to Harvard and the Shaker village with Hawthorne. It was true that the whole society seemed to be, though stupid, cleanly and industrious. However, this shaking of their hands before them, like the paws of dogs, as they shuffled in their religious dance, suggested the last possible aberration of the mind. His fellow men could hardly appear to less advantage than in such senseless jumping. And when they talked on their outstanding topic, which they were very ready to do, there was such an exaggeration of the virtue of celibacy that one might think he had come into a hospital ward where all the invalids were afflicted with priapism!

Meanwhile, Lane, who wrote frequently for the periodicals, expressed himself in print on the subject of marriage and revealed the extent to which his zeal had carried him. Marriage as now constituted, he told his public, is not a universal act (his word to Emerson), but an individual act, and a selfish one. It is made the groundwork of the institution of property, which is itself the foundation of so many evils. Property must be abrogated in associative life, or it will be little better than isolate life. But it cannot, it will not be repealed so long as marital unions are indulged in, for up to this very hour we are celebrating the act as the most sacred on earth, and, what is called providing for the family, as the most necessary and holy duty.

In the presence of such circumstances, Mrs. Alcott, who had carried her ample share of the burdens at Fruitlands, was not quite at ease. In Lane's view, she was merely an expansion and enlargement of her husband's self, a nature in which, he thought, her children shared. If she went so far as to participate in this belief with him, Mrs. Alcott herself was certainly not in agreement when Lane asserted that marital union was commonly used to justify every glaring and cruel act of self-acquisition. Indeed, already in late November, Lane complained that she had given him notice that she intended to leave, she and her four children, and that she would take the furniture with her. He thought it hardly fair to be thus left in a new world naked and alone, but of course it would be impossible for him to remain with Alcott, for to do so would give him the unenviable reputation of having separated husband and wife.

And so it was that Fruitlands came to an end. Lane joined the Shakers for a while. He had made arrangements early in November to place his boy with them, and now, in January, he, too, went across Still River.

XII

For Alcott himself these latter days of crisis had been a period of great unhappiness. Nothing had more engrossed him these many years than his wish to participate in a grand revision of the thought of his age. It was true of him what Emerson had said—that he more than any other man was the cause of the communities which had sprung up in America to provide a new pattern for living, and that none who wished to speak on this subject could ignore him. Yet now his own particular scheme of a new social life was failing of realization, as he himself had begun to see in midsummer. The new world of hope which had opened to him in England among his admiring friends, the actual return with him to America of Wright and Lane, and, finally, the solid acres of Fruitlands beneath his feet— all these had seemed assurance that at last his magnificent dreams, his most unselfish wishes to be of service to the world, would not be in vain. No wonder now that he was despondent. No wonder that his associates marveled at the strength of his self-denial or complained of the rigidity of his asceticism or of what they regarded his arbitrary or despotic manners. What he had so long wanted was so nearly in his grasp and yet was slipping away. To avoid losing Lane and therewith the last physical prop of his vision of a social regeneration, he was almost willing to sacrifice the very things that he had once most treasured. One night in December, when Lane was in Boston, the father and mother and the older Alcott children had had a long talk. There were tears then, and later the little girls cried in bed—and prayed God to keep them all together.[14]

XIII

Emerson had once thought of his friend as realizing the pictures of the old alchemists: standing and brooding month after month on the very edge of a discovery of the Absolute. But now Alcott acknowledged that he was at the end of his quest, and that the great secret might be forever beyond his reach.

For Emerson it was very sad to see Alcott thus driven to the wall, reproaching men and wondering whether he should not reproach the gods themselves.[15] The world, Alcott had almost decided, was not a possible place for him to live in. He had been a lover of law, had tried whether law could be kept in this world, and all things had answered, No. He had entertained the thought of leaving the world, and if he should be found tomorrow at the roadside, it would be not his fault, but the act of the world. For Emerson this view of things was full of exaggerations and warped by Alcott's wearisome personalities. It was true that Alcott enlarged the known power of man, as was said of Michelangelo, and doubtless he was a majestical figure, looking easily along the centuries to find his equals, with a painful sense of being an orphan and a hermit in the present world. If only he were good-humored, not so tedious and prosing and egotistical and narrow. Under the circumstances, his statement proved too much: it was a *reductio ad absurdum*. There were fatal omissions in his view, but Emerson concluded that he should never attempt to set him right any more.

DEAR AND COMELY FORMS

THE YEARS THAT immediately followed were for Emerson strangely variegated, a mosaic of colors rather than a pattern of balanced shapes.

There were many days of serene happiness. The garden and the lawn about his house had grown. Acres had been added to the south, toward Mill Brook. He had bought the heater-piece, the triangular plot of ground in front of his house, between the Cambridge Turnpike and the Great Road. Along the shores of Walden he had purchased wood-lots, so that he might walk on his own land, beneath his own pines, and provide his own fuel. When he had first occupied the Coolidge place it had needed trees to make it seem comfortable and homelike. Now the trees that he had planted had flourished, and in the firs by his study windows he could watch the birds that came there—the oriole, the cedar bird, the warbler, the robin, and the rest. On spring and summer mornings, after breakfast, he loved to walk in his orchard, watching the growth of his pear and apple trees, examining the insects with which they had to contend, pruning the branches.

Nor had he become a householder who enjoyed merely the calm of pastoral scenes. The old unspoken pleadings of nature still sounded in his ears, still filled him with wonder and delight. At Nantucket, where he had gone one spring to lecture to the fishermen, he had stood on the seashore to watch the play of the Atlantic with the coast, every wave reaching a quarter of a mile along the shore as it broke. What a wealth of strength that might be used to save the limbs of human toilers! And with all this power, what freedom and grace and beauty! As each billow rolled in, the breeze blew back the foam like a woman's hair in the wind. Such freedom made man seem a slave; such majestic movement dwarfed his expression to something slight, and thin, and cramped. Could not such a scene teach man a generous eloquence? The sound of the sea and of the wind was the disciplinary Pythagorean music which should be medicine. The witnessing of so excellent a spectacle—was it not a certificate that all imaginable good should yet be realized? He would scarcely have dared believe that such beauty existed. What, after this, might not be certified in the actual beholding of a hero or a noble woman?

Some of his pleasures in nature he was sharing now with Ellery Channing, who had married Margaret Fuller's sister Ellen, and who had moved into the red cottage on the turnpike below Emerson's. To Ellery, nature seemed prodigal of beauty. As the friends drifted at sunset in their boat on the river, Ellery had only to strike the water with his oar to show Emerson such an opulence of color as he had never seen before. The eddies were a hue of Rhine wines; they were jasper and verd antique; they were gold and green and chestnut and hazel in bewitching succession and relief without cloud or confusion. And still, as Ellery and he on late September afternoons sat on the steep hills of Conatum, to the west of Fairhaven Bay, they shared their old regret. Should all this beauty perish? Was there none, was there no way, to remake this sun and wind, the sky-blue river; the river-blue sky; the yellow meadow spotted with sacks and sheets of cranberry pickers; the red bushes; the iron-gray house with just the color of granite rock; the paths of the thicket; the cattle grazing on the hills? Shakespeare had seen no better heaven or earth than this, and it needed only a skill like his to save this beauty, this present moment.

The season rolled on, however, and brought new scenes and new pleasures. Once they walked to Carlisle by the old road in the region of the limekiln and the Estabrook farm, a country made up of vast orchards where apples grew in profusion, and where no hedges were wanted, the wide distances being fences enough. Barberries flourished at the roadside, and grapes along the walls. Here were varieties of apples not found elsewhere, the Tartaric and the cowapple, as Ellery said. They were of a kind which Emerson remembered from his boyhood, each containing a barrel of wine and half a barrel of cider—the touch-me-if-you-dare. They seemed to grow for their own pleasure; they almost lost price. The ground was strewn with them in red and yellow heaps—a rich and mellow autumnal bounty.

II

These years left Emerson with a new awareness that he was growing older. The days seemed rarer now, more precious. They came and went like muffled and veiled figures sent from a distant, friendly land, saying nothing, but offering gifts, and stealing silently and accusingly away when he did not take what they had to give. It struck him with strange interest when some of his friends remarked that they could not credit that they were already as old as their predecessors when they had died. Of the possibilities of his own death he had thoughts, too, but forewarned and without alarm. When the summers came, he saw how fast they matured, how short they were; but after the heats of July and August, he felt reconciled, like one who had had his swing, to the cool of autumn. So it would be, he thought, with the coming of death; and hence with such meditations, which visited him frequently now, he had long ago made his peace. He had awakened one morning and reflected that after more sleepings and wakings he should lie on his bed sick; then, dead; and through his gay entry his friends would carry his bones. Where should he be then? He had lifted his head and beheld the spotless orange light of the morning beaming up from the dark hills into the wide universe.

Alcott had said that as we grow older the beauty steals inward. That was one way of saying that our penetration increases as we grow older, that we are no longer deceived by great words when unrealized and unembodied, that we detect littleness in expressions and thoughts that once we should have taken and cited as proofs of strength; that was saying that as we grow older we acquire some patience, some temper, the perspective to rank our experiences and to know what is eminent. With maturity, in short, we may hope to attain character. And what could be more commanding than character? The matter was never clearer to Emerson than when old Dr. Ripley had died, at the age of ninety, and Emerson had gone to see the body, a handsome and noble spectacle, it had seemed to him. Yes, a man was but a little thing in the midst of the great objects of nature—the mountains, the clouds, the cope of the horizon, and the globes of heaven—yet was not here present evidence that a man by moral quality may abolish all thoughts of magnitude, and in his manners equal the majesty of the world?

III

Unhappily, not all days saw for Emerson an equal composure. He admitted to himself sometimes that life in large part is a succession of moods. Character, indeed, is regular and homogeneous. But we do not live an equal life, but one of contrasts and patchwork; now a little joy, then a sorrow; now a sin, then a generous or brave action. If anything were but true two days! One day we think ourselves the Angel Gabriel and the Archangel Michael combined, with sword or spade or pen capable of opening the secret caverns of the universe. Who but we? But next day we whistle and are speculative, and have a profusion of common sense. Resistance is good, and obedience is good, but who under heaven knows how to mix the two? Our approval of one or the other is all retrospective. Life is a puzzle and a whirl, and the cards beat the best players!

That is, Emerson was admitting doubts.[1] He was saying that the depth of our moments of faith may indeed constrain us to ascribe to them more reality than to all other experiences, but that our vice—our doubt—is, after all, habitual. Though within us is the soul of the whole, the wise silence, the universal beauty, we nevertheless live commonly in succession, in division, in parts, in particles. Two thirds of life—we may as well admit it—is dullness or pain. Nor must we regard these as Sunday objections, made up on purpose to be put down, for with these hobgoblins every superior mind must contend. These skepticisms keep returning—the suspicion, for instance, that it is fatal to earnestness to know much. There are times when knowledge seems a knowing that we cannot know. The dull pray; the geniuses are light mockers. And who has not suspected that even the lawgivers and the saints are infected by doubts—that they found the ark empty; saw, and will not tell? Worst of all, has there not been a cloy or satiety of the saints—their confession that, in the midst of their vision, their beatitude has been but partial and deformed, and that they must fly for relief to the intellect, itself so capricious? What refuge then in a world in which all things seem to swim and glitter? This is the midworld in which the ancients lived, a universe the possession of gods discursive, fickle, unpredictable. What refuge but the refuge of the ancient stalwarts—the Ulysses—the will to endure? In the long intervals between the moments of faith and insight in a world of incalculable experience, this, perhaps, remains the best stay: Never mind the ridicule, never mind the defeat; up again, old heart!

IV

Once, at church, he had felt how unequal is the match of words against things. What right had the unauthorized talker to prate, in neat and balanced sentences, of consolation, and resignation, and spiritual joys? Below the preacher sat those to whom care and calamity were *things,* and who looked up for somewhat to fit their case. What for the preacher, then, but to speak things, or to hold his tongue? And then once again since the death of Edward and Charles and Ellen, he, too, in the midst of many untroubled or happy days, was to know care and calamity and doubt. What of solace could he say when his own individual world suddenly shattered in a seemingly patternless experience? It had been this event, more than the later fiasco of Alcott at Fruitlands, which had caused the restlessness of these middle years of his life.

He and Lidian had been married a little more than a year when their first child, a son, had been born. Emerson thought it a blessed child, a lovely wonder that made the universe friendly to him. He was Pygmalion now, though he could see nothing in the child of himself. He was no conscious party to any feature, any function, any perfection he beheld in it. He seemed to be merely a brute occasion of its being, and nowise attaining to the dignity even of a second cause. How remote from his knowledge, how alien, yet how kind, did his son make the Cause of causes appear! What was most beautiful was to see the babe and the mother together, the contrast of size making the little nestler appear, it seemed to the father, so *cunning*. The tiny beseeching weakness was compensated so perfectly by the happy patronizing look of the mother, a sort of high reposing Providence toward it, that the two made a perfect group.

There were childish illnesses, and the father uttered anxious, spontaneous prayers that this sweet symbol of love and wisdom might be spared to rejoice, and teach, and accompany him. It appeared that the boy would not be strong. And yet he prospered, and was the center of family interest. Father and mother facetiously called him Little Pharisee, because, when he fasted, he sounded a trumpet before him. Lidian was the baby's interpreter: Hair, said little Waldo, is divine to pull; moreover, mamma is a porridge-pot, and pap is a prime horse. When he had learned to coo, it was like a pigeon house, Lidian said; and when he had learned to laugh, Emerson was cheered. It was a hearty and protracted laughter, and reminded the father of the pleasant thunder in the woods. They liked to watch the child play with the lamp shadows on the wall, though they agreed that there never was a baby so lovely but that even his mother was glad to get him asleep.

When he was a little less than a year old, Waldo stood alone for the first time, as the father recorded in his diary between references to the poetry of Ben Jonson and remarks on Sidney and Hampden. Then Waldo walked alone, and soon the whole house was his domain. One afternoon early in spring Lidian came into the study, where her husband was, as usual, writing in his rocking chair, and found the towerlet that Wallie had built, half an hour before, of two spools, a card, an awl-case, and a flower-box top, each perpendicularly balanced on the other. She could scarcely believe that her boy had built the pyramid! In a fit of affection she threw herself on the floor by the structure and kissed it down, and declared that she could possibly stay no longer with papa, but must go off to the nursery to see the lovely creature, and so departed. It was apparent that Lidian was fond of her boy. When Waldo was almost two, she took him, one summer day, to see old Dr. Ripley, across the village at the Old Manse. Waldo had come home with a present in each hand—two apples, which he refrained from eating until he was nearly home. Lidian must show her husband where the little angel had gnawed them. They were worth, she said, a barrel of apples that the boy had not touched.

Even as his son grew older, Emerson remained tender toward him. Though Waldo was permitted in his father's study, that sanctum was not the boy's favorite place for play, as the father noted with some pangs of disappointment. When Waldo looked out of the study windows, the view of the woods, he told his father, did not please him as did the woods he saw from the window of the nursery. But they—father and son—were good companions nevertheless. Once, when a circus came to town, they went together and saw a trained horse carry a basket in its teeth, pick up a cap, and select a card out of four. The boy, however, did not like the clown; the funny man, he said, made him want to go home. During the father's solitary walks in the woods, too, thoughts of his boy were often in his mind. One day as he walked along twirling his stick as he liked to do, he came upon the drollest September mushroom, tall, stately, pretending. Such ostentation *in petto* he had never seen. When he threatened to crush it with his stick, it seemed to plead piteously with him not to burst the fabric of its pride. He could almost hear Waldo begging him, as when he had menaced his little block-house, not to pull it down! And so, after due admiration of this blister, this cupola of midges, he left the little scaramouch alone in its glory. Sometimes, also, though Waldo was now scarcely five, he accompanied his father to the woods near Walden Pond. Later, Emerson remembered seeing the boy, when he came to a tuft of violets in the wood, kneel down on the ground, smell of them, kiss them, and depart without plucking them.

Then, within a handful of days, when Waldo was only a little more than five, he was stricken with scarlet fever and died. It was, the father recorded in his diary, at fifteen minutes after eight on the night of January 27, 1842, that Waldo gave up his little, innocent breath like a bird. The next morning, after a snatch of sleep, Emerson awoke at three o'clock to hear every cock in every Concord barnyard shrilling with the most unnecessary noise. The sun went up with all his light, but the landscape was dishonored by the loss of this boy. When the father arose to still his beating mind in a walk about his yard, every article in the house reminded him of his boy—the microscope, the magnet, the little globe, and every trinket and instrument in the study. Out-of-doors, the woodpile suggested the armfuls of wood which Waldo had carried for his grandmother's fire; in the barn were the hammer, the pincers, and the file he was so eager to use; in the henhouse were the nests from which he had gathered the eggs. The doghouse, the garden—everything spoke of Waldo. Down at the bottom of the garden, where it edged Mill Brook, it seemed as if someone had fallen into the water. As the day advanced, every tramper that ever tramped was abroad, though two little feet were still.

Sorrow, Emerson reflected, destroys all differences of intellect, and makes us all children again. The wisest knows nothing. When he had returned from the lecture engagements which could scarcely be canceled, he found dear friends at home, but not his wonderful boy. The chrysalis which Waldo had brought in with care and tenderness for his mother to keep was still alive, but he, the most beautiful of the children of men, was not. This beloved boy—how he expanded in his dimensions, in memory, to the dimensions of nature! But of the experience of Waldo's death, Emerson confessed that he comprehended nothing but its bitterness. Explanation he had none, consolation none that arose out of the experience itself; only diversion, only oblivion of this, and pursuit of new objects. Winter and spring had gone, and the delicious days of mid-June had drawn him to Walden Woods again before he could contemplate his loss with some equanimity. Then, as he had sat in the arm-chair of the upturned root of a pine tree, reading the manu-script of a deeply religiously-minded friend, he had felt for the first time since Waldo's death some efficient faith again in the repairs of the universe, some independency of natural relations whilst spiritual affinities could be so per-fect and compensating.

But the wound did not quickly heal. This was a calam-ity which he could not easily conquer, which experience would not assimilate, and which made him restless for years. It was long before he could look at the event calmly, though at last even these brutal facts lost their terror. Long after-ward, when Sleepy Hollow Cemetery had been laid out among the wooded hills along the new Bedford Road, Emerson had purchased a burial lot there. It was then that he had Waldo's remains removed from the grounds where the boy had been buried beside old Dr. Ripley, on the hill where the revolutionary church had stood overlooking the village center. Before the coffin had been put into its new vault and covered with slabs of granite, he had had it opened, and he had ventured to look in. It was a day early in July, and the morning sun shone brightly. Emerson plucked some white-oak leaves and strewed them on the coffin. Waldo had been dead fifteen years.

v

It had been the death of Waldo which had begun the restlessness for Emerson as he entered the period of his forties. Then the turn of events at Fruitlands, and his fear that he should not again enjoy his old sense of companionship with Alcott, did much to disturb his customary tranquillity. But there were still other disappointments, still other irritations which, added to these, were a part of the mosaic of these years.

There were, among other things, his imperfect relations with Thoreau. In the year before Waldo's death, Henry had been engaged to help with the household tasks—in the garden, where he and Emerson worked together day by day, in the poultry yard, in the orchard, in odd jobs about the house. In such tasks Henry was of the greatest assistance. But he was often, in hours of leisure, a delightful companion, too. Emerson was forever grateful to Henry for having introduced him to the riches of the shadowy, starlit, moonlit river, a lovely new world lying as close and yet as unknown to the trite one of streets and shops as death to life, or as poetry to prose. Henry had taken him, one afternoon in early June, through only one pasture to the river and the boat. Then they had left all time, all science, all history behind them, and entered into nature with one stroke of the paddle. About them was an enchanted liquid, painted with all imaginable reds and purples and yellows, which glowed under and behind them as Henry rowed into the sunset. Presently the stars came out and began to cast such ineffable beams as to stop all conversation. Then the moon rose and cleared the clouds. As Henry rowed swiftly along, and so caused the moon to go, now pure through her amber vault, and now through masses of shade, and now half-hid through the plumes of an oak or a pine, each moment, each aspect of nature, was suffi-cient and perfect. The moon, the hill, the tree, the air became but animated geometry and numbers. To them there was no intemperance, for they were born through law and had ripened and ended in beauty. Only man, through the transgression of law, sickened and aged.

Emerson remembered with gratitude, also, after the death of Waldo, how Henry had charmed the boy by a variety of toys—whistles, popguns, boats, and all kinds of instruments which he could make and mend; and how he had won Waldo's love and respect by the gentleness and firmness with which he always treated him. Emerson was pleased by Henry's verses, too, though he thought that Henry had not yet made the thyme and the marjoram into honey. But some of Henry's offerings for the *Dial* were full of his old fault of unlimited contradiction: his praise of wild mountains and winter forests for their domestic air; snow and ice for their warmth; villagers and woodchoppers for their urbanity; and the wilderness for resembling Rome and Paris. With all its merits, such writing made Emerson nervous and wretched. Furthermore, as he told Henry him-self one day, his writing did not disclose new matter. With all of Henry's thoughts he was quite familiar—they were his own, quite originally dressed. But as for any new ideas that Henry had thrown into circulation, he had not yet told what he was created to say. Though, unlike Alcott, he was to be admired for declining all the kingdoms of this world in spite of his great practical faculty, he remained, nevertheless, only another grand promiser; he had not yet acquitted his debt to society. And with Henry's running amuck against the world by refusing to pay a tax, which was mainly owing to the village, because he opposed the principles with which the government was entering a war with Mexico—with Henry's opposition on the basis of such a fractional issue, Emerson had no sympathy. It was, he confided to Alcott, a mean and skulking act. Thoreau appeared to him sometimes only as a *gendarme,* good to knock down a cockney with, but without that power to cheer which makes the value of a friend.[2]

Disappointing to Emerson in these years, too, were his associations with Charles Newcomb, whom he had met at Providence on one of his lecture tours after the death of Waldo, and whose conversation and written tales greatly pleased him at their first meeting. It was, indeed, the reading of Newcomb's manuscript, on that June day when he had sat among the upturned roots of the pine tree, which had first restored some of Emerson's faith in the universe after the loss of Waldo. At Brook Farm, where Newcomb had gone to live, and where Emerson had visited him, Emerson found Newcomb a quiet, retreating, demoniacal youth, greatly respected there, and exercising a sanitary, retentive influence. He was not a person to be seen on a holiday or in holiday places, but one should live in solitude and obscurity with him for the only person in the country to speak to. Emerson saw him only infrequently, but always, in these first years, with increased admiration. Once when he had gone to see him he had found him, as always, wrapped in his great Gothic cathedral of fancies, but pained now by the doubt of whether he should retire to a more absolute inward priesthood, or accept the frequent and to him dear solicitations of domestic and varied life. Saints in a convent who all recognize each other, and still retire— that was his image. Never was a purer service to the intellect offered than his—warm, fragrant, religious. Emerson thought him beautiful and dear, one whom God and all his hosts must necessarily keep.

And yet now, in the midst of other disappointments, somewhat more than five years after Waldo's death, Emerson felt a dissatisfaction with Newcomb, too. What a fathomless skeptic this San Carlo was! Thought he defied, and regarded it as noxious, because it makes us old, harried, and anxious. The defect in his friend's view, it seemed to Emerson, was that thought is no more to be declined than hands and feet are. Thought is like the weather, or birth, or death: we must take it as it comes. Moreover, thought is work which, like every work, reacts powerfully on the workman, for out of this anxiety flows a celestial serenity. Alas, it seemed to Emerson that his friend had become the spoiled child of culture; the roué of art and letters; blasé with too much Plato, Dante, Calderón, and Goethe; so fearful of losing the level of life that he had written nothing for years. Newcomb was like a man afraid to bring an armful of wood from his shed for fear that he would injure the balance of his mind. Emerson confessed that he himself had learned a sordid respect for uses and values, and that he must have them. And so, in his diary, at least, he bid this once beautiful genius farewell. If, in later years, he learned to think otherwise, at present it seemed to him that Newcomb, like Alcott and Thoreau, was only another promiser actionless in a world that demanded performance not only for the sake of the world, but for the sake of the doer as well.[3]

With himself, however, Emerson was at this time no less impatient than he was with his friends. The reason why he had insisted on the exemption of the writer from all secular work—in the days when some of his friends were urging him to join Brook Farm—was his conviction that the scholar's work needs a frolic health to execute. He had long recognized, moreover, that he could not live as many others did. It was only by the most exact husbandry of his resources, he was sure, that he could attain the health and spirits necessary to accomplish anything. Now, in this period of numerous disappointments, he was more than ever convinced of what the doctor had told him in his boyhood—that he had no stamina. If only he might have the right kind of society, if only he could talk with people who would stimulate him![4] Perhaps any stated task might provide the stimulus that he felt he needed. He recalled now that all his mature life he had wished in vain for a professorship—that even an offer from the plainest country college would have pleased him. Much as he disliked the ministry as an occupation, he could almost welcome a pulpit as a means of rescue from the doldrums in which he now found himself. One of his friends had recommended an abolition campaign, and Emerson had agreed that a course of mobs would probably do him much good. His own inclination was to go to the vast solitudes of Canada, there to withdraw himself from all domestic and accustomed relations and thus—for a time—to command an absolute leisure with books. But in the end he thought it best to yield to the request of some English admirers to deliver a considerable number of lectures in England and Scotland. And so, after fourteen years, and for reasons somewhat similar to those which had taken him from home in 1833, Emerson left a second time for England. He sailed from Boston for Liverpool on the packet ship *Washington Irving* on October 5, 1847.

VI

For Alcott, the months immediately following the breaking up of Fruitlands were among the darkest of his long life. The waters of the flood seemed to remain endlessly upon the earth, and the family endured as best they could until a wind arose and the windows of heaven were stopped. They lived for a time in the village of Still River, and then took rooms at the home of Edmund Hosmer, Emerson's farmer friend, at the outskirts of Concord, on the Lincoln Road, somewhat more than a mile from where Emerson lived. In the winter of the first year after Fruitlands, Emerson, it seems, offered to help finance Alcott if he and Lane should again wish to join forces in community life. Though Mrs. Alcott was apparently not unwilling to cast her lot once more for such an endeavor, Lane declined. Their friend Emerson, he protested, was not acting, nor did he profess to act, wholly on universal grounds. It was not earnest devotion and unquenchable hope that his offering suggested, but merely the purest individual friendship. With a venture inspired by such private and individualized motives, Lane cared to have nothing to do, for such motives, he felt sure, would vitiate and mar, if not entirely neutralize, the good moral results which should be their aim. He should not find his salvation by living with the Alcotts on such worldly terms as Emerson's offer presupposed.[5]

At this juncture, fortunately, Mrs. Alcott came into a small legacy with which she purchased the old house at the head of the winding lane once the main track of travel before the turnpike branching off from the old Boston road by Emerson's door had been built. There was an acre of ground with the old house, which had had a varied history since its beginnings in pre-Revolutionary War days, and across the Great Road; in the meadows, lay a half-dozen acres or more which Emerson purchased for the use of his friend. In these scenes Alcott busied himself remodeling the house, cutting terraces in the steep hill which rose almost directly at the rear door, planting an orchard on the terraces and across the road, making a garden, setting out willows along Mill Brook where it flowed under the rock bridge down the lane. He prided himself particularly on the rustic arbor which he built on the hillside somewhat to the west of his house. In the shadows of its thatched roof and its lattices of hemlock and willow, he enjoyed sitting during the heat of a summer's day or in the dusk of evening. Below, to the south, he could see the meadow where his orchard and garden lay, and beyond, to the southwest, the ancient wood which hid Walden Pond. It seemed appropriate to call the new home Hillside.

Alcott had not resigned himself without a struggle to the life of a gardener on these acres. He had hoped to teach in Concord, yet even the little primary school, across the road from Emerson's front door, had been denied him. Were there, then, no avenues open to the sympathies of his townspeople? Why should God refuse him to be useful to his fellow men? Might he not be permitted to use his gifts for his neighbors' children, if not for themselves, and thus aid the coming, if not the present, generation? How long should he thus be tried by this exclusion? To what ostracism did not the frank declaration of his opinions sometimes drive a candid and thoughtful man! Nevertheless, he was thankful that his own children were still within the reach of his influence, and grateful that the kindness of friends had made it unnecessary for him to beg bread for his children's mouths or raiment and shelter for their bodies. Once again, as in those almost desperate days when he had searched for employment in the machine shops of Boston, he sought what solace he could in his poverty. Blessed was poverty if it made him rich in gratitude and left him a temper that railed at none! Besides, deep within himself he had not given up hope. Even though the world had accepted as teachers of the time the men in whose circle he had moved—Emerson and Garrison and Carlyle—and had ignored him, he was not bitter. For him the world was perhaps not quite ready. His day was yet to come.

Alcott found much comfort, too, in his reading, for which, happily, this rural life as gardener left numerous hours in the day. He was much occupied, in the years immediately following Fruitlands, with Carlyle, whom he regarded as the greatest modern Englishman, perhaps the greatest living articulate man. Carlyle, he thought, had done more than any of his contemporaries to initiate a new era in letters, to open the well of German wisdom. And among the Germans, Alcott was engrossed in Goethe and Schiller and Richter—particularly in Goethe. It was one of the auspicious signs of the time that so many of the best of American youth had turned to the reading of Goethe. But most profoundly interesting of all was his reading in Oriental literature, especially the Bhagavad-Gita. This poetry and philosophy of the Orient seemed to him superior to if not transcending greatly all other literatures. It was intellectual, serenely pure, and spiritually sane.

He had lived at Hillside almost a year when he drew his courage together to look once more at the manuscript of his own "Psyche." Now, after all these years, it seemed again a living word. With corrections, it was a book worthy of printing, though the criticisms which Emerson had made long ago still seemed, for the most part, true and just. Though he could not think of Emerson's old criticisms without pain, against Emerson himself he bore no ill will. Indeed, for Emerson's present writing he had the most lively zeal. He had read some of the poems which Emerson was preparing for the press, and they had convinced him that his friend was America's first truly western poet, as Occidental as our forests and hills. These poems, together with the earlier essays, gave Emerson a place with Goethe and Carlyle, were the best evidence of the growth and ripening of an American man. Emerson's writing was bold, clear, profound, and graceful. It had not, indeed, the sharp and polished definiteness of Goethe's work, nor the intense manifold boldness of Carlyle's, but it possessed a depth and serenity, an elevation and comprehensiveness, belonging to neither Carlyle nor Goethe. Its one outstanding trait that must commend it to all modern men was its infinite hopefulness. England and Germany, who had so long swayed the world, had now, in Emerson, found a rival on these Western shores.[6]

Now that he was back in Concord, Alcott found himself gradually returning to his old personal relations with Emerson, though the freshness of their intimacy, alas, he recognized had gone. The Fruitlands episode, which had come as a barrier between them, Alcott found too painful to talk about, though Emerson had offered to reunite him with Lane. But they saw each other frequently, sometimes at Alcott's home, which was scarcely more than a half mile from Emerson's, sometimes at Emerson's study, and sometimes in walks to Walden Wood or around the triangular piece of meadow that lay between their houses. Emerson came most often in the spring or summer evenings, at which time the friends sometimes sat in the rustic arbor on the hillside. At such times Alcott spoke of his readings in Goethe or in the poetry of the East, in which Emerson had read since, when he was a boy at college, he had come upon the translations of Sir William Jones, and in which he was now finding the inspiration of some of his own poems. Emerson came one evening to show Alcott Carlyle's daguerreotype profile, which he had received a few days before from his English friend. Together they examined the shape of the head, the jutting brow, and the eye, in which Emerson thought he saw the strong executive talent which had made Carlyle's thought available to the world. Their talk ran to the genius of Carlyle, and drifted finally to Boehme's doctrine of signatures and the law of images and

sound. With Boehme, both had been long acquainted.
One evening Emerson quietly left ten dollars with which
he asked Alcott to buy paper for his journals. Alcott had
long delayed copying them for want of paper, and with this
gift he looked forward to the pleasant labor with which to
fill rainy days and Sundays and the winter season to come.
When Alcott returned these calls, the friends most often
sat in Emerson's study, where Emerson read many of the
poems which he was preparing to publish. There they
talked, too, of Thoreau's refusal to pay the town tax, a
refusal which Emerson thought in bad taste, though Alcott
defended Henry's act as a dignified noncompliance with
the injunctions of evil powers. In their Walden walks,
Emerson sometimes spoke of his plan to build a study
on the southern shore of the pond, and in the intimacy of
these paths so sacred to Emerson, Alcott ventured to ask
his friend to speak a word, during his lecture tours, in behalf of the conversations for which Alcott was again beginning to plan. At Walden, too, they sometimes visited
Thoreau, who was living there now in his cabin in the
woods.

With Thoreau, Alcott's acquaintance had become a
warm friendship, though the two had not first met auspi-
ciously. In the first years of his intimacy with Emerson,
Alcott had visited at Concord for several days early one
May, now almost a decade ago, and had accompanied
Emerson to the Thoreau home, where a group had gathered
for a conversation. Emerson had not been satisfied, said
the people were stupid, and that Alcott had not met them
wisely. Alcott had thought little of the event, at the time
did not even know how to spell Thoreau's name. But now,
in Henry's second year at the pond, he and Henry were
cordial companions. Especially on winter days, when his
gardening tasks were at a standstill, he was a frequent

visitor at Thoreau's hermitage at Walden. On one unforgettable evening Henry had read him some passages from his manuscript volume entitled "A Week on the Concord and Merrimac Rivers." Alcott thought the book purely American, fragrant with the life of New England woods and streams, a book which could have been written nowhere else. Particularly was he touched by Thoreau's sufficiency and soundness, his aboriginal vigor, as if a man had once more come into nature, a man who knew what nature meant him to do with her—Virgil, and White of Selborne, and Isaak Walton, and Yankee settler all in one. Alcott had come home at midnight through the snowy wood-paths and had slept with the pleasing dream that presently the press would give him two books to be proud of—Emerson's *Poems* and Thoreau's *Week*.[7]

In these contacts with his friends, Thoreau and Emerson and others, Alcott felt that he was fulfilling, at least in part, his old ambition to move the living times. Though a directly active participation in a new age seemed denied him, it was some compensation to be with Emerson and Thoreau when they met at Emerson's or at Boston to discuss, for instance, now that the *Dial* was no more, the possibilities of a new and purely American magazine. On such occasions he might meet on an equal footing those who were the moving instruments of the day—Theodore Parker, Charles Sumner, Frederick Hedge, George Ripley, W. H. Channing, James Freeman Clarke, and others. It was a great pleasure and privilege to participate in the ideas which were stirring men, ideas which would soon be planting institutions. The delight of these meetings seemed the pledge of issues both grand and national. It was, however, in his solitary walks and conversations with Emerson in Walden Wood that Alcott most clearly felt that his life was not in vain. At the end of an afternoon at Walden, when he parted from Emerson at the turnpike and entered the little green lane on his homeward way, he could not but feel more vividly than before the rare privilege he enjoyed of passing at once from the busy and painstaking toil of the week into the presence of Emerson, and gaining admittance, as a friend, to the first thoughts of this first great American poet.[8] It seemed to compensate for his rugged lot, the best, doubtless, which the benign yet equitable Disposer could yield to him in justice to the imperfect use which he had made of his talent and opportunity.

Although he was not obsequious in Emerson's presence, Alcott was fully aware, in these years, that his hopes had not prospered as had those of his friend. In the earlier confidence of his own future success, Alcott had once questioned whether Emerson possessed that persistency of will which vanquishes the hindrances of fortune. Now, in the ebb of his own affairs, he was wholly willing to grant that his friend had no want of stern discipline. If at this time he did not feel that he was the stimulus to Emerson that he once had been, was no longer Emerson's peer, he was without bitterness or jealousy. He was perfectly willing to meet his old friend on whatever honest grounds, however humble; therefore he was pleased when Emerson, who had enjoyed the hillside arbor, came to consult him about a lodge that Emerson intended to build on the peak of his woodlot near Walden Pond. They walked to the woods together, and Emerson pointed out the ledge on which he intended to build a hut for study and writing. The prospect, Alcott agreed, was commanding. Monadnoc was toward the north, and westward and southwestward, Wachusetts and the shires of Acton and Sudbury. Over Fairhaven Hill lay the Sudbury River, and northward, across Walden Pond, Henry's cottage—altogether a fit spot for a poet's lodge.

But in the end the plans for the lodge were abandoned,

and Alcott was employed, instead, to lay out the grounds for an arbor on Emerson's lawn, southward from the house, and somewhat back from the turnpike. Thoreau helped, too, and together, early in June, they set out pines and hemlocks around the site of the bower, with some large firs near where the doors were to be. Later, in mid-July, Alcott and Thoreau and Emerson himself carried their axes to the Walden woodlot and cut down for posts of the arbor twenty hemlocks—trees, as Emerson remarked, which had been growing while he was sleeping—fenced, bought, and owned by other men, and now, in this new want of his for an ornament to his grounds, their care, and the long contribution of the great agents—sun and earth, rain and frost—supplied this rich botanic wonder. The work was for Alcott a task of love. There were many trips to the woods, trips on which his daughters accompanied him sometimes, to gather curiously twisted sticks and branches for the latticed windows or for the rustic lyre emblazoned above the door, or moss for the decoration of the seats. On rainy days he sat with Emerson awhile, or took his tools to the grinder. He seldom reached home from his work till quite after dark. Then, after a supper of cream and honey and wheat cakes, with apples and peaches, he still found himself pursuing his charming occupation to bed, and, all through the night long, in happy dreams. When morning came, and he arose at five, it was with an eagerness to resume his toil as soon as the family chores were done. Then he was at Emerson's again with hammer and saw. The arbor was not yet completed when Emerson, on the Sunday eve before his departure for England, came to say good-by to Alcott, and left him fifty dollars.

There was yet another tie, simple yet strong, which now bound the friends together, a tie, though of another nature, perhaps as firm as those intellectual aspirations which they

had shared as a common hope in the first years of their
friendship. Though Waldo was gone, there were other
children in the Emerson household now—Ellen (whom
Lidian had named) and Edith and Edward. As for the
Alcott family, the father had resolutely put from his memory
all recollections of the temptations of Lane and the Shaker
ways, and all were living as quietly and with as much content as at any former period of their lives. Anna was very
much interested in the study of German and French, and
Louisa, as her father said, while she inclined toward no
specific study, yet gave promise of a ready genius for whatever she pleased to undertake. Elizabeth, a gentle and faith-
ful creature, accomplished lessons at school or in house-
wifery with equal skill and readiness. She and May were
spending a part of each day at Emerson's, where Miss Ford
had a little school in the barn for the Emerson children.
There were simple studies and needlework, and walks to
Walden Pond, and botany lessons in the fields and woods.
There were festive occasions, also, as at Fruitlands, when the
parents joined the children in idyllic pastimes. In the second
spring at Hillside, on the first of May, Alcott had trimmed a
wagon with running pines, and then all, children and
parents, too, with pine wreaths upon their hats and bonnets,
had driven over to Emerson's, singing as they went,
"Merrily we go." On Emerson's lawn the children danced
around a Maypole which had been gaily dressed with ever-
greens. On summer Sundays, Alcott came frequently with
his younger girls, and out in the yard under the trees
read the parables to the children, with conversation and
much original matter woven into the text. Emerson and
Lidian often joined in the conversation. Louisa, too, helped
with the teaching of the Emerson children. She was in her
early teens now, restless and full of moods. She was
happiest running in the woods before the dew was off

the grass—on the hills above the Alcott house, where she could see the sunshine over the wide Virginia meadows. In Emerson's library, where she often browsed, she had read *Goethe's Correspondence with a Child;* so she wrote Emerson letters (which she never sent), left wild flowers on his doorstep, and sang Mignon's song under his window:[9]

Kennst du das Land, wo die Citronen blühn?

Indeed, it was largely upon such homely, such simply human grounds that the friends now met. According to the external facts, the facts which the world could see, Emerson was now an essayist, a poet, and a lecturer of some renown, of fame enough to have his writings published abroad, as well as at home, and to be invited to England for a lecture tour—a novel honor for an American. Though he was not wealthy, his property had increased, and he was able, by innocent and indirect devices, to give aid to his less materially fortunate friends—Channing and Thoreau and Alcott. Alcott, on the other hand, was a small gardener, with four children, and in straits. He was almost forty-eight, and his hair was gray. At first glance, as Thoreau wrote to Emerson in England, when one looked at his gray hairs his conversation sounded pathetic. When one looked again, one was reminded of the gray of dawn; and when one listened again, it was clear that Alcott was the youngest man of his age—just on the threshold of life![10] At present, however, it appeared that he had failed, and that he had to content himself with that mid-world which Emerson, too, in another way, had discovered. No wonder then that he was happy to walk in the dark lowland meadows, though, for Emerson, the sun was now on the tops of the hills.

VII

In England, before the first of March, Emerson had delivered dozens of lectures in the north and in Scotland.

For three weeks he lectured almost every evening in Liverpool or in Manchester. There were lectures, too, in Derby, Sheffield, Nottingham, Birmingham, Preston, Leicester, Chesterfield, Worcester, and elsewhere. At Edinburgh he gave a new lecture on which he had been working at odd moments during his tour, "Natural Aristocracy," a challenging title in that land. In Glasgow he spoke in a cavern called the City Hall to some two or three thousand people. There were excursions also to Perth and Dundee, and then a return southward to Newcastle-upon-Tyne. He tried to reconcile himself to the clatter and routine because he wanted to see men and things in a close and domestic way. But the lectures were often pounds of flesh, and he became disgusted with them and protested that he would read no more. More requests were made, however, which he could not refuse, and so he consented to drudge on a little longer. It was doubtful for some time whether he would lecture in London under circumstances which he cared to accept, though at last, after almost a month's absence in Paris, he began, in the first week of June, a course of six lectures which took three weeks. He was not happy with this program because the London newspapers had so fully reported his northern lectures that he had to prepare new ones hurriedly, and he detested haste. Unfortunately the price of admission arranged by his friends for these lectures was high, and the audiences were relatively small; hence he yielded to a plea for additional lectures at a less expensive hall, at lower prices. But, in the end, his speaking tour in England proved financially unprofitable. People were too concerned about the current political and social dangers in England and France to be greatly interested in nonpolitical lectures. Emerson had borrowed $800 when he left Concord, and remained in debt almost $600 upon his return home in the last week in July.

Nevertheless, he had his wish to see many men, though perhaps not always in a close and domestic way. He met many contemporary celebrities, and was dined and entertained right and left by the high and the low. He saw Carlyle again and Wordsworth, met Dickens, Thackeray, Macaulay, Tennyson, Leigh Hunt, Milman, Alison, Lord Jeffrey, Lockhart, Collyer, Cruikshank, Jenny Lind, David Scott, De Quincey, Clough, Patmore, Matthew Arnold, J. S. Mill, Faraday, Richard Owen, Robert Chambers, Disraeli, Chopin, Harriet Martineau, and many others. He was dined at Lord and Lady Asburton's, at Lady Harriet Baring's; attended soirees at Lady Palmerston's, at Lady Morgan's, at Lady Molesworth's, at Lord Lovelace's, at the Marquis of Northampton's; was entertained by the Duchess of Sutherland, and at Samuel Rogers'. He was introduced to Prince Albert, Sir Charles Fellows, Dr. Buckland, Baron Rothschild, the Duke of Argyle, Lady Byron, Mrs. Jameson, the Bishop of Oxford; saw the Crown Prince of Prussia, the Prince of Syracuse, and many another whose name he could not even remember. In the fashionable circles he thought that he found the greatest simplicity of speech and manners, great directness, though perhaps an even greater want of high thought than in the society of Boston. He did not decline opportunities to see all this fashion and ostentation, because he wished to know how the other half lived, though he could not and would not live with them. And a very little of fashionable society was enough for him. The old deoxygenation and asphyxia that had always existed for him in the word "party" continued unchanged in London palaces.

When he had arrived in London on the first of March, the city had been agog with news of the late-February revolution in France—the fall of Louis Philippe and the rise of the Republic. Everybody was saying that Paris was no

longer Paris, nor France, France, but everything was *triste*
and grim. Emerson read the *Times* eagerly every day, and
heard about him expressions of fear that the fever might
spread to England, where the splendid privileges of the
palaces contrasted only too dreadfully to the common famine
and ignorance. In the restless days back home in Concord,
he had agreed with a friend that a course of mobs might
be good for him; now he determined that at all hazards
he must see Paris. The rumor that France might soon shut
its doors to all peaceful men only made him the more eager
to go and to hurry his departure. Tennyson, who dis-
trusted affairs in France, assured Emerson that if he went,
he would never return alive.[11]

By the end of the first week in May, Emerson was in
Paris. Such fire and fury, he reflected, would be incon-
ceivable in New England. All France was bearded like
goats and lions. Even the costumes were formidable, for
most of Paris was in some kind of uniform—red cap, red
sash, brass helmet, and sword; and everybody was thought
to have a pistol in his pocket. But the deep sincerity of
the speakers who were studying how to secure a fair share
of bread to every man and to get God's justice done through-
out the land was, he thought, good to hear. And so he
frequented the clubs which dotted the city and in which
there were loud and stormy discussions of the issues of the
day. He saw Barbès rule in his Club de la Révolution, and
Blanqui in his Club des droits de l'homme. He was present on the momentous fifteenth of May when the *rappel*
was beaten in the afternoon, when the streets were full of
bayonets and there was a furious driving of horses dragging
cannon toward the National Assembly. For several hours
it appeared that a new government would be declared, the
old routed, and Paris acquiesce in terror. But before night-
fall all was safe, and Emerson rejoiced that the ringleaders

of the extremists, Barbès and Blanqui, were secure in the dungeon of Vincennes.

Paris, Emerson decided, had great merits. The living was cheap and good. The manners of the people made it easy to live with them. Then they opened their treasures of art and science so freely to the mere passport of the traveler and to all the world on Sunday. A special advantage was the freedom from aristocratic pride manifest in the tone of society, the ease with which any young man of liberal tastes might enter on a good footing the best of houses. But all Paris, on the other hand, seemed to Emerson a continuation of the theater. Besides, life was cheap in this anthill, for it was clear that multitudes sold their future for the excitement of one day. Moreover, in the gay and admirable illumination of the Champs-Elysées, he thought he could see that France was but a few steps from socialism and the phalanstery. He remembered his old objections to Brook Farm: You shall not so arrange property as to remove the motive to industry. If you refuse rent and interest, you make all men idle and immoral.[12]

Back again in England, even before he had completed his June lectures, Emerson was ready to return home. He had seen what he had wished to see. For these Englishmen, who had been very kind to him, he had the greatest admiration and respect. Their substance seemed to be the best of the world. A manly ability, a general sufficiency, was, he thought, the genius of the English. Their manners revealed a genuine independence. They were castles compared with Americans. In their company an American must feel like some invalid. And yet, when he saw the tragic spectacles which the streets of the great manufacturing cities had to show, the poverty, the beggary, the drunkenness, the prostitution, he could not regard these matters without some terror, or without reflecting upon the safety, the opportunity, and the dignity which were so easily obtained at home. England, he had learned, was the country of the rich. Once, in his journeys, he had observed that his coach traveled twenty-three miles adjacent to one man's property. The owner and his friends, in red hunting coats, were returning from hunting with hounds, and met the coach on the road, their horses and dogs very much spent. No, England was very different from America. At home, on the Fitchburg Road between Boston and Concord, he might board the cars and see sweltering men take their seats with well-dressed men and women and note but little difference of level between them all. How astonished the polished inmates of English first-class carriages would be if such masters should enter and sit beside them! America was the Paradise of the third class; there everything was for the poor. England, essentially aristocratic, was the Paradise of the first class; there the humbler classes contentedly entered into the system. In England every man you met was some man's son; in America, he might be some man's father.[13]

The one Englishman whom Emerson had wished to see more than any other was Carlyle. Fourteen years before, when they had walked over the hills in Wordsworth's country and their conversation had been of the immortality of the soul (Ellen had not long been dead), his visit with Carlyle had come to an unsatisfactory close. But there had been a friendly correspondence in the interval, they had been helpful to each other in the publication of their works, and they remembered only the pleasures of their first meeting. Therefore, when he had arrived in Liverpool late in October and discovered that he had a week of freedom before his lectures began, Emerson eagerly accepted Carlyle's invitation to Chelsea.

It was ten o'clock at night when Emerson knocked at the

door of Carlyle's suburban London home. Jane opened the door, and behind her in the hall, with a lamp in his hand, was Carlyle himself. They were very little changed, Emerson thought, from their old selves of fourteen years before when he had left them at Craigenputtock. Carlyle was ardent and voluble. The floodgates of his talk were quickly opened, and the river rushed forth in a plentiful stream. There they were, he said, shoveled together again. They had a wide talk that night until nearly one o'clock, and again next morning when they breakfasted at nine. At noon they walked to Hyde Park and the palaces, about two miles to the National Gallery, and to the Strand, Carlyle melting all Westminster and London into his talk and laughter as he walked. He was an immense talker, and as extraordinary, it seemed to Emerson, as in his writing. Without seeing him, one could have no adequate conception of his real vigor and range, or how much more he might do than he ever had done. Emerson perceived that his few hours' discourse with Carlyle, long ago, in Scotland, had not given him a sufficient knowledge. Now, at last, he thought that he understood him truly.

Carlyle was not mainly a scholar, but a very practical Scotchman, such as one would find in any saddler's or iron-dealer's shop, and then only accidentally and by a surprising addition the admirable scholar and writer that he was. His guiding genius was still what Emerson thought it even before he had seen the man on the first trip to Europe—his perception of the sole importance of truth and justice, his hatred of cant. He was impatient of literary triflers, and contemptuous of *Kunst,* whether of German, English, or American variety. The English Parliament, with its babble, he denounced. It was difficult, however, to be patient with the sneers and scoffs which he threw in every direction. He broke off every sentence with a scoffing laugh

—almost everybody was, in his judgment, a windbag, a monkey, a donkey, or a bladder, and speak of whom he would, it was always "poor fellow." Though he agreed that many listened to him and admired him, he protested that not one had the smallest intention of doing what he said. When Emerson chided him for undervaluing the many worthy people who surrounded him, Carlyle said he prayed the beneficent gods to defend him from ever sympathizing with the like of them! The four days of his visit had not yet ended when Emerson wrote in his diary that he should not readily find better or wiser men than his old friends at home. Carlyle, he was sure, would never satisfy them or begin to answer the questions which they asked.

Nevertheless, after his return to London from his lectures in the north, Emerson did see Carlyle again, though not often or with much pleasure. Once, late in April, they dined together, with Dickens and others, at Lincoln's Inn Fields, and the conversation turned on what Emerson regarded as the shameful prostitution of London streets at night, which seemed to him to betoken a fatal rottenness in the state. Carlyle admitted the condition but seemed unconcerned. Yes, he heard whoredom in the House of Commons; Disraeli betrayed whoredom, and the whole House of Commons revealed universal incontinence in every word they said. Chastity in the male was as good as gone. In England it was so rare that he and Dickens could name all the exceptions. He supposed that the same was true in America. When Emerson protested, Dickens said that incontinence was so much the rule in England that if his own son were particularly chaste, he should be alarmed, as if he could not be in good health. Leigh Hunt, said Dickens, thought it indifferent.

Carlyle, it was clear, was no idealist. It was curious, the magnificence of his genius and the poverty of his aims.

He drew his weapons from the skies, but only to fight for
some wretched English property, or monopoly, or prejudice. It appeared that he was a protectionist in political
economy, an aristocrat in politics, an epicure in diet, and
went for money, punishment by death, slavery, and all the
pretty abominations, though he tempered them with epi-
grams. Among his friends, he would listen only if you
declaimed to him as he declaimed to you. He did not care
to see anybody whom he could not eat, and reproduce, tomorrow, in his pamphlet or pillory. Alcott and Margaret
Fuller, when he had seen them, were meat that he could
not eat, and he rejected them at once. A short, plain-
dealing communication he did not care for. He had the
provincial traits of an islander and a Scotchman; he believed more deeply in London than if he had been born
under Bow Bells; and he was pretty sure to reprimand with
severity anyone who dared make light of the British islands.
He was, in short, an inspired cockney.

A week or so before leaving England, however, Emerson
enjoyed with Carlyle an excursion which relieved somewhat the growing tension. On the seventh of July, they
set out for Stonehenge, which neither had seen. Carlyle's
local knowledge of Hampshire, as they rode the train to
Salisbury, made the way short. From Salisbury to Ames-
bury they drove by carriage, and the remaining distance,
some seven miles or so, under a gray sky, they walked. But
even the pleasure of this excursion was threatened when the
conversation drifted to the subject of Americans who
traveled in England. Carlyle complained that Americans
disliked the coldness and exclusiveness of the English, who
had much to teach them, and ran away to France to be
amused. Though Emerson himself had only recently returned from a month in France, he had gone to see a revolution, and not to be amused. Carlyle's remark, neverthe-

less, looked much like a personal thrust; but Emerson ignored the implications and assured Carlyle that he was easily dazzled and would readily concede all that any Englishman would ask. He liked the English because they could do everything; but, meantime, he knew that as soon as he returned to Massachusetts, he would renew the old conviction, which the geography of the country inspired, that America played the game with immense advantage; that there and not in England was the seat and center of the British race; that no skill or activity could long compete with the natural advantages of America, in the hands of the same race; and that England, like other parents, must one day be contented to be strong only in her children. With this proposition, however, Carlyle would not agree.

Fortunately, the sight of Stonehenge itself was a common interest. On the broad downs, not a house was visible, nothing but Stonehenge. A few shepherds sprinkled the plain, and a peddler drove along the road. They walked round the stones and clambered over them, to accustom themselves to their strange aspect and groupings, and found a nook sheltered from the wind where Carlyle lighted his cigar. It was pleasant to see that this simplest of all structures—two upright stones and a lintel laid across—had long outstood all later churches and all history. Within the enclosure of the mounds grew buttercups, nettles, and, all around, wild thyme, daisy, meadowsweet, goldenrod, thistle, and the carpeting grass. Overhead, larks were soaring and singing.

It was twilight when they left the mounds, and in showers of rain they walked the two miles to their inn. Late as it was, men and women were out trying to protect their windrows. In showery England, Emerson observed, the grass grows dark and rank.

In spite of the partial reconciliation with Carlyle in the

solitude of Stonehenge and the pleasures of a holiday excursion, Emerson was heartily glad to return home. His homesickness and his dissatisfaction with the circumstances of his travels had been progressive. Even on the sea voyage bound for England, he wrote Lidian, pictures of home rose before his eyes as he lay in his berth at night. The children he could see plainly. One night he distinctly heard Ellen call him to come to her. Then, presently, in England, there were letters from home. Henry, who was in the Emerson household managing affairs, wrote about the latest activities in the poultry yard, in the orchard, about the doings of Hugh the gardener, of Alcott and the arbor, about the routine of picture-seeing every night with the children before bedtime. Lidian was often ill. There were some difficulties with family finances that Emerson had not been able to foresee. Should they ask Alcott to repair the well-sweep?

When he had had his first disappointment in Carlyle, Emerson wrote Lidian that he should never be tempted from home again unless he should find better things than he had found. To Margaret, who was in Italy, he wrote that it would give him no pleasure to bring his friends from home to England, though he should have a lively pleasure to bring Englishmen to Concord so that they might see his friends at home, in their own place. When he had letters from Henry and Ellery, early in December, he confessed that they had grown dearer by distance, and—though he hesitated to say it—by comparison. In April, Lidian wrote of the present which Mrs. Alcott had given Eddy. Lidian enclosed the letter that Mrs. Alcott had sent with the gift. It was perfect in its kind, Emerson thought. Only people who had hearts could write letters so tender and beautiful. And Alcott himself had been making a picture book for

Eddy! It made him fearful when people were so kind to
such a stone as he was!

But, more than anything else, more than the routine of
lecturing, the tedium of parties, the shocking street life of
the big cities, the gross inequalities of European society and
the false remedies—more than any of these, it was the
hardness, the skepticism, the negative attitude of those he
found in Europe which repulsed him and made him long
for home. The one thing most odious to him was the sneer-
ing joke. He could not avoid thinking of Carlyle, for what
could the brave and strong genius of Carlyle himself avail,
if, whether one fell or whether one rose, there still followed
the inevitable joke? If the English people owed to their
House of Commons this damnable derision, they had paid
an overprice for their liberties and empire. For himself,
Emerson preferred the noble companions whom he had
left at home, who valued merriment less, and virtues and
powers more. When he balanced the attractions of good
and evil, when he considered what facilities, what talents, a
little vice would furnish, then there rose before him, not
these laughters, but the dear and comely forms of honor and
genius and piety in his distant home.[14]

<h3 style="text-align:center">VIII</h3>

It was good to be back in Concord. Emerson resolved that
he would never travel again—at least not until his children
grew up and forced him to do so. The day after his return
Alcott came to spend the morning and to listen to the experiences abroad. In the evening of the next day, Emerson
called on Alcott, and there was more to say of the great
journey. When Emerson had to leave, and many things
still remained unsaid, Alcott walked home with him along
the old path, under the dark elms and sycamores, where
they had walked so many times since Alcott had lived at

Hillside. At Emerson's they found Elizabeth Hoar and George Bradford and other townspeople who had come to welcome the returned traveler and to hear the tale of his adventures. And so these summer days and nights passed in pleasant reunion, in eager conversation on subjects new and old.

When Fruitlands had collapsed, Emerson had never been more conscious of the fatal omissions in Alcott's views, and he had felt that he should not again try to set him right. It had not been easy to be patient with Alcott in those days, not easy to forget the conviction that Alcott was unlimited, unballasted—a pail without a bottom. But more and more, as time went on, he had become assured that it was false to say that Alcott was quite impracticable, however hard it was to deal with his thought, which was so incompatible with the opinion of the Boston *Post*. It was true that although Alcott looked at everything in larger angles than any other person, the apexes of his angles were never quite defined, and thus lacked the attribute necessary to true greatness. It was true that he could not write, that in the attention to the marshaling of his written words the thing marshaled dwindled and disappeared. It remained true, also, as Ellery said, that Alcott's egotism was always an obstruction. You first had to kick the man away in order to get at what he knew. But even before his departure for Europe, Emerson had had his faith renewed. Nothing, Alcott had said one day, is more indicative of the deepest culture and refinement than a tender consideration of the ignorant. What was most agreeable in that assertion, Emerson thought, was the wealth it indicated in Alcott's nature. An ample culture had he and to spare.

Now, after his return home, Emerson could see more clearly what he himself had once said—that love reduces all inequalities, all differences, as the sun melts the iceberg in the sea. Friends such as we desire are dreams and fables. Friendships that we have in flesh and blood are not solely intellectual, nor can they give perfect accord. Besides, here was Alcott reading his old favorites again—Pythagoras, Plato, Jesus, and—Pestalozzi! The past and the old ties renewed themselves as Alcott spoke again of some of his old convictions—that the soul is older than the body, that a teacher is one who can assist the child in obeying his own mind, that anything in Plato can be drawn from any group of well-selected children. In his school in Boston, when he had made the schoolroom beautiful, he had looked on the work as half done. A friendly biography of Alcott, Emerson thought, might begin with that passage in the *Republic* in which Plato speaks of those who by instinct can trace out the springs of grace and beauty; for such a man was Alcott.

Now, too, after his return home, Emerson was able to tell wherein his indebtedness to Alcott lay. It seemed clear now that Alcott was a certain fluid in which men of a certain spirit could easily expand themselves and swim at large, they who elsewhere found themselves confined. He gave them nothing but themselves, and of course he seemed to them the only wise and great man. Yet when they met people of another sort, critics and practical people, and were asked concerning Alcott's wisdom, they had no books to open, no doctrines to impart, no sentences or sayings to repeat, and thus found it quite impossible to communicate their good opinion. It was in this fashion, Emerson saw, that Alcott had served him for twelve years and more. Alcott was the one reasonable creature whom he needed to speak to.[15]

IX

It was sad that Alcott was moving to Boston. His friends were beginning to value each other, Emerson ob-

served, now that Alcott was to go. Ellery declared that he
never saw that man without being cheered, and Henry said
Alcott was the best-natured man he ever met: the rats and
the mice made their nest in him. But that was only Henry's
manner of speaking when he was among Concord friends.
He had not forgotten how Alcott had come from the village, through snow and rain and darkness, till he saw the
lamp in the Walden cottage, and shared some long winter
evenings with him. Alcott was a blue-robed man, his
fittest roof the overarching sky which reflected his serenity.
To converse with him was a New England Night's Enter-
tainment.[16]

THE LONG LEVEL YEARS

THE ALCOTTS WERE abroad in the world again upon the quest of their fortune. The gardening of her husband not proving adequate to meet the increasing family needs, Mrs. Alcott ventured to take the helm—for a time serving as a visitor to the poor (the still poorer!) for some benevolent societies in Boston, and then establishing an employment agency and keeping boarders. Anna and Louisa taught or did housework for others, while Beth kept house at home and May went to school. One summer they all had small-pox, the father and mother and the four girls, and Alcott and his wife were very ill. They had no doctors, no nurses, no visitors. In this period Louisa published her first story—something that she had written in Concord at the age of sixteen.

Within seven years, the hopes which had taken them to Boston had vanished, and the family moved to Walpole, New Hampshire, to live in the house of a relative, rent free, where Alcott could garden again. It was a lovely place, Louisa thought, a little house in a lane, high among the hills, with a beautiful ravine where she could walk or run. The smell of the fresh earth and the touch of the green leaves did her good; besides, there were pleasant people and good neighbors, plays and picnics, busy and happy times for all, though no essential family problems had been solved, except that the older girls were able to help now. Louisa was writing and publishing more and more, with rising ambitions to be a noted and well-paid author.[1]

The struggle and the pathos of this family drama Emerson viewed with a growing indignation against the nature of things, and with a surer conviction of the merits of his friend. It seemed to him a bitter satire on the social order, this plight of Alcott, the most refined and the most advanced soul in New England, a man of such courtesy and greatness, that, in conversation, all others, even the intellectual, seemed sharp, and angry, and fighting for victory. Was it any real discredit to Alcott that he had the least shop value of any man? Because he could not earn money by his pen or his talk, or by schoolkeeping or bookkeeping—indeed, for the very reason that he was ahead of his contemporaries, and kept himself out of the shop-condescensions and smug arts to which the successful resorted, it was the unanimous opinion of New England that, should he die, all would hear of his death with pleasure, and feel relieved that his board and clothing were saved! How far better, really, were Alcott's outward shiftlessness and insensibility to what society reckoned the primary claims, than the Bulwer view of intellect, as a sort of bill of exchange easily convertible into fine chambers, and wines, and cigars.[2]

And so, when it became clear that the Boston hopes were vain, and Alcott came again to ask advice—whether to try his lot as itinerant conversationalist or to resort once more to country gardening—Emerson favored the latter as the surer venture. He did what he could, also, in protecting Alcott from his own incredible unworldliness; consequently when, in the midst of this dire present poverty and hopeless outlook, Alcott proposed to go to England to investigate his genealogy and apparently had actually secured funds from some of his friends for that purpose, Emerson interceded and diverted the promised funds, as well as securing additional ones, for an annuity for the partial support of Alcott's family. It was, he acknowledged, a very bad precedent to release a man from the duty of taking care of himself; yet Alcott's case was extraordinary and exceptional. Among the things that go to make up the world, there might well be one Capuchin or divine mendicant, and Alcott had unique claims as being the abbot of all mendicant orders. Besides, Alcott was never to hold the whole fruit in his hands, but was to be permitted to bite only an annual berry. Under these circumstances Emerson contributed $100 to the annuity and obtained equal or lesser sums from some of his friends—Longfellow, and Lowell, and others.[3]

Alcott himself, however, was not idle in his attempts to find a vocation that would at once provide a livelihood and permit him, as he had phrased it, to move the spirit of the times. He still pinned his hopes on the success of the conversation, and to this end busied himself upon the family's arrival in Boston. A characteristic theme for an evening's conversation was "Enthusiasm, or Abandonment to the Instincts," in the course of which he read from Swedenborg and Pythagoras, and from the poems of Quarles, Milton, and Emerson. He offered a course of conversations on the "Reform Spirit of New England," his subjects being Webster, Garrison, Theodore Parker, W. H. Channing, Margaret Fuller, Emerson, Dr. Channing. Emerson joined him, early in these efforts, in two conversations which were advertised as a Parliament on the Times by Messrs. Alcott and Emerson, to begin at half-past seven o'clock and to close at ten precisely.

His enthusiasm for the conversation led him, with some encouragement from Emerson, to try an attack upon the West; indeed, in the autumn of 1853, he ventured as far as Cincinnati. It was with misgivings that Louisa, a young woman now, saw her father depart—he so poor, so hopeful, so serene, and so helpless in a money-loving world. Nor were her fears unjustified. Alcott returned one February night hungry, tired, dirty, cold, and disappointed—to be surrounded by his nightgowned wife and four daughters, all hovering and brooding over him, and all longing yet hesitating to ask the all-important but fearful family question, "Had he been paid?" Alcott had to confess that his overcoat had been stolen, that many promises had not been kept, that traveling was costly, and that in his pocketbook he had exactly one dollar. But he had opened a way, he thought, and would do better another year.[4]

Emerson saw these latter adventures of his friend with mixed emotions. It was plain to him that Alcott was totally destitute of any lucrative faculty, so far as had yet been discovered. He was a little amused at some aspects of the conversations themselves—at the mad contradiction of seeing people who sympathized with engineers and gold-rushers, and who had come to the meeting on the cars, by steam-ferry, and by locomotive—of seeing such people solemnly meet to discuss their own breath, to speculate on their own navels, with eyeglass and solar miscroscope, and no man wondering at them. It appeared to him that at some of the conversations each person who opened his lips seemed in snuffing the air to snuff nitrous oxide, and away he went—a spinning dervish—pleasing himself, but annoying the rest. Each rode his nag with devotion round the walls of the universe. He himself found no benefit in such jar and jangle.

As for Alcott's part in these performances, Emerson had divided opinions too. Certainly Alcott was not always at his best, a main difficulty being that he could never finish a sentence, but revolved in spirals until he was lost in the air. On the other hand, Emerson was sometimes struck by his friend's superiority. The interlocutors were all better, at first, than Alcott, who seemed childish and helpless, not answering their remarks aright, while they were masters of their weapons. But by and by, when he got upon a thought, like an Indian seizing by the mane and mounting a wild horse of the desert, he overrode them all, and showed such mastery and took up time and nature like a boy's marble in his hand as to vindicate one's highest hopes of him. In his best talks, he ran up and down the scale of powers with as much ease as a squirrel the wires of his cage, and was never dazzled by his means, or by any particular; and a fine heroic action or a poetic insight made no impression on him because he expected heroism and poetry in all. Never was there anyone—and this was his greatest virtue—who so fortified the believer or so confuted the skeptic.[5] After one particularly happy evening, when the company had gone, Emerson praised the meeting and assured Alcott that the conversation was a power and must become an institution. No remark could have made Alcott happier or given more strength to his hopes.

Strangely enough, though perhaps his conversations were providing all the social contacts that he wished, Alcott was less desirous of meeting his leading contemporaries than he had been when he had first returned to Concord after Fruitlands, and when it had been some compensation for his restricted lot to meet with Parker, and Hedge, and Clarke, and others. It is true that, with Emerson, he was largely instrumental in the organization of the Town and Country Club, which first met in his rooms, and of which he was made secretary. Emerson noted, at the first meetings of the club, that Alcott was festal and Olympian when the friends gathered—that his heart seemed too great, that his voice faltered, and that every newcomer seemed to him large, sacred, and crowned. Emerson hoped that the club would afford an opportunity to debate important questions, that it would be dignified with literary exercises, and that some day it might have as many as five hundred or six hundred

members. But aside from meeting there an occasional intimate friend like Lowell, Alcott soon expressed his disappointment with the club. Though he granted that opinions
were never, at any former period of the world's history,
circulating with such speed and momentum and pure tendency, he cared less for association with others than at any
other time. He was, for one thing, much too occupied with
writing to wish for the pleasures of a club. He had a recipe,
it is true, for *mixing* human enjoyments: for disputation,
crowds; for rumination, the woods; closets, for thought; and
for discourse, a single friend. But just now thought and
rumination and discourse were paramount in his desires.

Never, it seemed, had his thoughts been more pleasant,
sweeter, a greater solace, or livelier, than in these years.
There were, first, the old theories of genesis or creation
which had begun with his reading in Plato and the Platonists, and were now receiving new color and animation
from his study of Swedenborg and the Goethe and Oken
morphologies. Once, in September, he came out from Boston
to Concord to spend some weeks to renew his health in the
country air. He stayed at the Hosmers', who owned and
lived near the little cottage which Alcott had occupied during his first residence in Concord, and from his windows he
could see the garden grounds which he had once tilled,
and the cottage itself, where his youngest daughter had been
born. On this visit, there were sweet nights of sleep and
dreams, and, after an early breakfast, walks along the railway, over the hills near Thoreau's deserted hermitage, along
the clear, cool Concord, and in the invigorating sunshine
and the morning moisture; then, hours of immersion in his
books and papers in the delicious endeavor to put into form
his latest thoughts on Oken and Goethe. It was, later, with
pride that he recognized his own ideas in Emerson's published essay on Swedenborg.

It was in these years, too, that he heard Emerson deliver his course on "The Conduct of Life." The "Fate" he regarded as a brilliant performance, Emerson himself being the best illustration of his theme, the victor of the fate which he celebrated so royally. The "Wealth" pleased him less well. Finer things might be said in praise of poverty, though it would take a person superior even to Emerson to say them. Thoreau was the better man to celebrate that estate concerning which he knew so much, and which he wore as an ornament about himself. But, still later, when Emerson's *English Traits* was published, Alcott was stirred as he had not been in years. This, he thought, was a book of which England, Old and New, might well be proud. It was a victory of the eyes over the coarser senses, and a triumph of idealism over the current idolatries. Platonism, since Plato, had not before gained such full ascendancy in any mind. In this volume Emerson had represented the new philosophy, and for the first time celebrated the cosmopolitan spirit of America and its independence of the mother isle.[6]

In the year of the appearance of *English Traits,* Alcott had, too, the exciting experience of meeting Walt Whitman, an extraordinary person, he thought, full of brute power, genius, and audacity, and likely to make his mark on young America. Alcott shared with Whitman the conviction that the best thing our country had done was the growing of Emerson. If only a broader and finer intercourse with men would serve to cure Whitman of his arrogance and egotism, Alcott expected great things of him—this representative man and poet of America.[7]

But it was not the hopes for literature engendered by Whitman, or the pleasures of his reading, or even the delight in his own writing, from which Alcott was now receiving his greatest sustenance; rather it was from discourse—from

talks with individual friends. During his seven years at
Boston mainly, but also during the two at Walpole, he made
many trips to Concord, and on such occasions he never failed
to see his old companions. There were Sunday-morning
saunterings with Thoreau, and discourse as they reclined
on the grass in the Indian meadows near the river. Moreover, there were innumerable walks to Walden with Emerson, to swim at the cove on warm summer days, at night
sometimes to see the stars reflected in the water, or, perhaps,
to discuss the demonic in nature and mankind, while the
rain poured and they walked drenched in wood and pasture. These days and nights in Concord with Emerson,
in study and field, besides Walden Pond and Wood, were
distinguished by nameless traits from all other days and
nights in Alcott's calendar of experiences. There was
nothing like them, nothing comparable; they made conversation and ideas possible, the pleasures of friendship without
stain. Rather than actual scenes on *terra firma,* they seemed
like sallies into some fabled cloudland, remote and golden,
where minds divested of mortal forms sat sedate and aloft,
discoursing free

On fate, free will, and foreknowledge absolute.

Such days, such conversations, had about them something
planetary and astral, and showed the proper place of our
little planet in the solar system.

A difficulty was, after such occasions, that it took Alcott
a day, and a night's sleep, to restore him to his place and
poise for the customary round of life. Besides, from these
conversations, there remained nothing reportable, though
they were not lost, but, like some ray from the old stars,
still blended with evening and morning twilights of his
experiences. There remained always, however, the conviction that in the friendship of the incomparable Emerson

he had the friendship of the master mind of his country and of his time.[8]

Concord was classic land. There lived the men whose names would one day render Harvard and Yale, with all their professors and spacious buildings, ridiculous. Alcott felt, sometimes, that he was the richest man in the commonwealth in possessing such friends—Emerson, and Thoreau, and Channing—and Hawthorne, too (now back in Concord again, a famous author). These men he esteemed as the victories of his life, for they were country and countrymen, and their lives and places and times stood for thoughts and things perennial and enduring. In Concord he partook more of the home sentiment than anywhere else. Here there had culminated experiences as memorable as instructive. The cottage, its acre and the idealities it had sheltered; the English Iliad half-realized, with its sequel of Fruitlands' idyls and nameless weary woes; then Hillside with its bucolics; Emerson, Thoreau, and the hermitage; Channing's wild walks and talks; the *Dial,* Greaves's library, and Charles Lane—all these attached him to Concord and left him the hope of returning to what was his truest inheritance under the sun. And this hope became a deep longing one Sunday in May when he and Emerson and Ellen and Edward walked through the new cemetery at Sleepy Hollow, Emerson pointing out his family lot, still rudely staked on the Pine Grove mound. For the first time, then, Alcott breathed aloud his wish of reclining some time, near Emerson. It would be a sweet and calm repose to be thus not far from his benefactor and the friend of whatever was imperishable in him.

II

Emerson had begun his career as lecturer upon his return from his first visit to Europe. He had spoken in Boston, and then, later, in other New England towns and cities.

By 1842 he had been as far abroad as New York City. In the summer of 1850, in a long journey westward to the Mississippi, he spoke in Ohio, and, a few years later, in Michigan, Wisconsin, Illinois, Iowa, and Missouri. Though he disliked traveling, he was, nevertheless, in his own country, probably one of the most widely-traveled Americans of his day.

When, in the 1850's, he first ventured into what was then little more than wilderness, he was, of course, not unknown. He had been lecturing in the East for seventeen years, he had received wide publicity for his lecture tour in England, and he had published several books, among them a volume of poems. His reputation, in short, was already established: he was by the best-informed people regarded as the foremost, if not as the sole, American scholar. There were even those who believed that his poetry, because of its freshness and originality, was among the best in America and would live when the popular verse of Longfellow had fallen into hopeless neglect. As a lecturer, certainly, his reputation placed him at the very top of the list; he, more than anyone else, was a pioneer in the profession, and had done more than any other one man for its dignity and elevation.[9]

But when the lecturer himself appeared, to be seen for the first time, his Western audiences were not always sure that the man before them was the one of whom they had heard. Emerson was a tall man, full six feet high, but slender and bony, and in his plain suit of ill-fitting black looked, to some of his audiences, not unlike a New England country schoolmaster or a sensible farmer, rather than a philosopher and poet. His face was thin and strongly modeled, his nose large, his eyebrows arched and meeting. When he was introduced, he approached the lecturer's stand with an appearance of embarrassment, half apologetically.

and, while he spoke, scarcely ever looked his hearers in the face.

Those whose standard of public speaking was that of the popular elocutionist of the day regarded him as no orator. To such, he seemed to read his manuscript without excitement, scarcely even with emphasis. His few gestures, if not positively awkward, had all the qualities of Yankee stiffness. But more discriminating judges saw his greatness gracefully disguised under his sincere modesty. To them his baritone voice was marked by an exquisite modulation of tone and emphasis. He read with a calm, classical power and dignity, and every intelligent listener was drawn by his words. When he occasionally looked out over his audience, his blue eyes, they observed, could be terribly keen and piercing.

The task of lecturing in the West, and all that it meant in those days of primitive travel, Emerson himself accepted as one of the obligations and opportunities of his life. He had once spoken caustically of the notion that the scholar should be a recluse, a valetudinarian—as unfit for any handiwork or public labor as a penknife for an axe. Action, he had maintained, is for the scholar subordinate, but essential, and without it he is not yet a man. The attractions of the world which lies wide around are the keys which unlock man's thoughts and make him acquainted with himself. Only so much of life as he knows by experience, so much of the wilderness has man vanquished and planted, so far has he extended his being, his dominion.[10] Emerson himself ran eagerly into the resounding tumult.

The inconveniences and the hazards of travel in the new West were sufficiently numerous to satisfy the most zealous craving for experience. Since the lecture season extended mainly only through the winter months, Emerson knew at firsthand the bitter cold of the prairies when the temperature had dropped to the lower twenties, knew what a cold, raw country it was when he arrived at four in the morning to take the last and worst bed in the tavern and when the only refuge in the unheated room was to hasten under the covers. He knew the hazards of crossing rivers on the ice or at fords when there were no bridges, and the danger of rowing across the Mississippi when the ice was breaking and the biting wind purpled the skin and numbed the fingers. He knew the terror of cholera and death in the river towns. He had experience with January thaws and the bottomless mud of wilderness roads. He drove fifty miles in a buggy to deliver a lecture and another twenty afterward to make connections for the next day's travel. Once when broken rails precluded travel by train, he met his lecture engagement by driving sixty-five miles through the snow in a sleigh, and remarked only in his journal the words of a settler to whom he had spoken that in Michigan the world was done up in larger lots.[11] When the mid-winter temperature rose to normal, there were halcyon days, he thought, and the hundred miles of forest through which he rode were gay and vernal. He was a seasoned traveler.

When he had lectured in England, he had met the literary élite and the social aristocracy—princes and lords; now, in the West, he was seeing the makers of a new country. He saw the businessmen who were developing the apparently boundless resources of the wilderness; the professional men from the East who had come to seek their fortune; the land speculators; the gamblers; the cardsharpers; the well-disposed, kindly, and sinewy farmers, who sometimes walked out of his lecture rooms. He gossiped with tavern-keepers in prairie towns, and was amused, when he had spoken of the cold, to be assured that in Illinois they had no cold weather, but only now and then Indian summer and cool nights. He whiled away hours between trains at

railway stations, talking to telegraph agents and learning
with pleasure that a skillful listener can distinguish the oper-
ator by the accent of his dispatch, and that boys of sixteen
or so most quickly learn the work. He chatted with men at
livery stables, sat with the drivers on his long journeys, and
learned much about horses. The dwarfed and humpbacked
coachman who drove him from Kalamazoo to Grand
Rapids and back talked to the horses—and praised them—
all the way. "Ha, ha, Jimmy, what are you looking after?
Ha, ha, ha. Take care, Jimmy! . . . St! St! John! John takes
it easy, but whenever he's called on, he's on hand, ha, ha!"
The driver had slept nights for years in the same stall with
Sir Henry, a studhorse which had trampled and killed his
previous ostler. A barrel of sugar given to him first and
last had made him docile. Flora Temple, the humpback
told Emerson, had trotted for a purse of three thousand
dollars at Kalamazoo, and had made the shortest time ever
made in the Union, "two minutes, nineteen seconds, and
a half."

It was a magnificent spectacle, this panorama of the
Far West. The Far West, Emerson wrote to Carlyle after his
first visit in the upper Mississippi, was the proper name for
these verdant deserts. On all the shores, interminable
verdant forests. If you landed, there was prairie behind
prairie, forest behind forest, sites of nations, no nations.
The raw bullion of nature; what we call moral value not
yet stamped on it. The Ohio, it was true, was full of
boats, loaded to the water's edge, on their way to and from
New Orleans; but the great sweeps of the upper Mississippi
were lonely and awesome—the distance from the boat to
either shore, the unvarying character of the green wilderness on either side from hour to hour, from day to day—no
towns, no houses, no dents in the forest, scarcely another
boat in a hundred miles.[12] With all this spacious country

Emerson from year to year became better and better acquainted. He knew the great forests of Ohio, with their
immense black walnut trees, the oaks, the rock maples, and
the redbuds, and with their occasional clearings around log
huts and barns. He had been in Illinois, where the tall
prairie grass might conceal a horse and rider, and in Wisconsin, where the huge pines stood so closely together that
travelers had to use the streams. He had looked at the
waves on Lake Michigan in a bleak snowstorm and had
thought how difficult it was to represent such grandeur.
At Montreal he had watched acres and acres of ice rolling
swiftly down the St. Lawrence, making mad somersaults
and revolutions like porpoises in the water. He had been
at St. Louis, the Metropolis of the West, the very edge
of the frontier, the starting point for Sante Fe and California. With these material dimensions, their extent and
beauty, he was intimately familiar.

Emerson saw, too, the great game of speculation and pursuit of wealth which drew men to the West. At Galena, he
visited a lead mine which some poor farmer had stumbled
on when he went to clear a spring, and which in a few years
had yielded ore worth a hundred thousand dollars, and
would yield as much more. Chicago hummed with stories
of rapidly rising land values. The lot on which the American House stood had skyrocketed from $40,000 to $90,000
in one day. Emerson recorded in his diary the tale of the
New York speculators who bought some lots in Chicago—
in the swamp and woods—for $100,000, and within a year,
incredibly even to themselves, sold them for a million.
When he was in St. Louis a second time, after an interval of
two years, he wrote to his brother William of the wonderful
growth of that city and advised William that if he wished
to assure success to some young man of energy, St. Louis
was the place to send him. The far-reaching changes that

the new West might bring about in American society Emerson enjoyed revealing in the story of the Concord carpenter who, reading of the sale of building lots in Chicago, had said, "Can't hardly believe that any lands can be worth so much money, so far off." There were many things that the East was yet to see.

It was exhilarating—this boundless America. It seemed to give opportunity as wide as the morning. Emerson thought that its effect must be to change the peak of the mountains into a vast tableland, where millions could share the privileges hitherto in the hands of a few patricians. These endless acres and our national liberty were the nostrum of our country. And the Yankees who had taken possession of this vast territory had demonstrated that they could do anything as soon as it was certain to pay. But he welcomed the German settlers, too, who were leveling the forests and putting the land to wheat and corn. He welcomed them as he welcomed the Irish in the East, for it was the genius of America not to draw indiscriminate masses, but only the liberal, adventurous, America-loving classes of Europe. With such a people, America would be the idea of emancipation, the abolishment of kingcraft, of slavery, of feudalism, of unjust monopoly. What a political aid, too, was this invention of the locomotive which was to hold this vast North America together. Napoleon had overstated the case, it was true, when he had said that in twenty-five years the United States would write the treaties of Europe, but his words were nevertheless a prophecy.

And yet Emerson had to admit in his most careful thoughts that in America little or nothing had actually been attained. All was but gristle and preparation. Though he himself delighted in people who could do things, he saw that America was superficial, ignorant, and without real character. It was the vulgarity of this country to believe that naked wealth, unrelieved by any use or design, was merit. Our commerce was somewhat grand in its power, and the telegraph was grand in design, and already of immense benefit, but our politics were petty. We were, on the whole, a nation of shopkeepers. This rush to the West, too, was not altogether a sign of health. When a man went to California, Emerson thought, he announced it with some hesitation, because it was a confession that he had failed at home. Whatever might be said in favor of America—that its grand material dimensions could not suggest dwarfish and stunted manners and policy; that it inspired large and prospective action; that it meant opportunity, freedom, power—yet these instincts were not supported by adequate mental and moral training, and hence they ran into the grandiose, into exaggeration and vaporing. These circumstances were perhaps inevitable, but they were odious nevertheless.[13]

But it was not only, in these years, his lectures and travels in the West which drew him into the world of men and affairs. Even more stirring than these broadening experiences were the events which led him into a participation of the great questions of slavery and civil war. He had, indeed, lectured on slavery as early as 1837, and in 1844, against local opposition, had spoken in Concord on Emancipation in the British West Indies. He was reluctant, however, to throw himself into the question of slavery because he thought that whatever talents he had fitted him better for other ends. But when, in 1850, the Fugitive Slave Law was enacted, with Webster's support, he recognized that it was impossible to extricate himself from the questions in which his age was involved; he could no more keep out of politics than he could keep out of the frost. Here was a law which required him to hunt slaves, a law that disclosed

the secret of the new times, that slavery was no longer mendicant, but was become aggressive and dangerous. He
resolved that all he had and all he could do should be
given and done in opposition to the execution of the law.
He made no secret of his intention to keep people informed
of the baseness of their leaders.

Hence, in the ten years before the war, and during the
war itself, he publicly flayed Webster for his part in the
support of a despicable law, made speeches in the political
campaign of a Free-Soil friend, advocated the purchase of
the slaves from the South, and, four years before the war,
when Charles Sumner was physically attacked and injured
in Congress, proposed that it was time to raise soldiers.
When the Kansas question arose, he personally contributed
to the purchase of rifles for the settlers to defend themselves
against the border ruffians, spoke in behalf of the Free-
Soilers, welcomed John Brown at Concord, and, when
Brown was hanged by the order of a Virginia court, assured
his audience in a heated lecture that John Brown had made
the gallows glorious like the cross. With the election of
Lincoln, it seemed to him that the government had at last
a healthier tone, that the shame of living had been taken
away, though presently he grieved to see that the administration appeared to be following, not leading, and governed
by the hurrahs of the soldiers and citizens. In an address
at the Smithsonian Institution in Washington, D. C., he
advocated the immediate emancipation of the slaves—nine
months before Lincoln spoke the eventful words. And in
these efforts he not only entered a fray for which he
regarded himself ill-equipped; he was booed and hissed and
shouted off the lecture platform; he, the quiet scholar, had
to listen to cries of the mob: "Dry up!" "Throw him out!"
and the like. Lecture engagements were canceled, and he
suffered the abuse of proslavery newspapers. In these pub-

lic prints he was declared carnal-minded, insane; he was called a flunky, a fool, vermin, a cur; his reference to Brown and the gallows was labeled a blasphemous and traitorous sentiment; in short, his appearance on the lecture platform was regarded a public scandal.[14]

Emerson had, indeed, run into the resounding tumult. He had been in the world. He knew the appeals which the world makes to the materialist and the seeker after self-development; what questions, what doubts, assail the intellectual and impartial inquirer—the skeptic; what difficulties engage the idealist in his effort to honor, at the same time, the ideal, or laws of the mind, and fate, or the order of nature. The gamut of all these thoughts, of course, he had already run long ago in his essays on Napoleon, Goethe, Montaigne, and Plato. But if there had been anything of theory or knowledge rather than wisdom in his speculations when he had written *Representative Men,* his observations had found wide range in the intervening years, and his thought had matured in depth, and substance, and strength.

However, if he had been in the world, he had never really been of it. The multifarious experiences of these years of his maturity left certain fundamental convictions unchanged; he never became blasé with living. It was true, he admitted, that men in the street failed to interest him, because at first view they seemed thoroughly known and exhausted, as if he had taken an inventory of all their parts and qualities. But after the best count had been made, there really remained as much more, which no tongue could tell. It was this remainder with which the preacher, the poet, the artist were concerned, the region of power and aspiration. The best of truth is that which hovers in gleams and suggestions unpossessed before man. This chorus of thoughts and hopes, these dawning truths, like great stars just lifting themselves into his horizon, they are man's future, and console him for the ridiculous brevity and meanness of his civic life.[15]

III

In the meanwhile, while Emerson was thus in the midst of an expanding life of action, Alcott had returned to live at Concord. His thoughts had more and more been tending in that direction, and it had remained only for his wife and daughters to conquer their dislikes and go with him. Emerson's neighborhood would mean more to him than that of any other contemporary. Besides, Thoreau was there, and Hawthorne, who had bought Alcott's Hillside and was expected to return soon from his English consulate to rebuild and ornament his home. There was, too, Franklin Sanborn, a young and new resident, who had a fascinating scheme for a college at Concord, with Emerson, Thoreau, Hedge, Parker, Agassiz, and Alcott himself as teachers. And so, after consulting with Emerson and Thoreau, and Edmund Hosmer, Alcott had bought Orchard House and about twelve acres of garden and orchard and woodlands from John Moore, for $950. Emerson had gone security on a note for $450.[16] Since the buildings needed repairs and alterations, the Alcotts for the time being lived in a house near the Town Hall, while Alcott himself directed and participated in the remodeling of the old house which had been built in pre-Revolutionary War days, and which now stood shaded by some ancient elms, luxuriant and far-spreading. The estate was separated from Hawthorne's Hillside only by a gate and a shaded avenue, stood back a little way from the Great Road, and was only a short walk from Emerson's house. From his yard Alcott could still see the willows which he had planted at the rock bridge in the lane when he had lived at Hillside. It was along this Great Road and among the falling October leaves of these huge trees that he had first entered Concord to visit Emerson, now twenty-two years ago.

The arrival in Concord was saddened by Beth's fatal illness—scarlet fever, which she had contracted early in the previous year from some poor children whom her mother had nursed. She was but a shadow, and failing fast, when, in November, the doctor pronounced her case hopeless. Louisa was at home to take care of her sister, and watched with aching heart the suffering Elizabeth as she sewed or read or lay looking into the fire, all her pretty hair gone, and, at twenty-three, looking like an old woman, so tired and worn. On a day early in February, the father and mother had walked to Sleepy Hollow to find a burial spot for themselves and their children. The day was sunny, and smiled on their sad hearts as they thought of Elizabeth. On the Tuesday before her death, she lay in her father's arms, and, calling the others around, smiled contentedly and said, "All here!" Sunday she was gone. Emerson and Henry were among those who carried her to the plot in Sleepy Hollow which she herself had chosen. And so the first death had come into the Alcott family.[17]

Alcott continued his experiments with the conversations in the West; indeed, he had hastened home from such an expedition when it appeared that Beth must go. He called occasionally, during these tours, on people whom Emerson knew and whose names Emerson had given him, though he protested that he did not always find the qualities praised by his friend. Although he was able to come home with a little money now, he was thankful to leave the slovenly West and to return to what he called the civilities of Massachusetts. As he had walked on the levee along the Mississippi at St. Louis, seeing the steamers, the mound, the people, all novel and strange to a New Englander, he had thought how purely Eastern he was, how little he had in common with the wild life of the West. He seemed to be older than this wilderness, its rough ways, and looked about him in vain for the mankind, the landscape, of which he was part and parcel, as if he had been thrown upon these banks by some mishap and some centuries too soon.[18] He was of course not aware that the future was to bring him quite other views.

Like Emerson, Alcott too was watching the course of national history with keen interest. He himself, in 1854, had taken an exciting and dangerous part in the attempted rescue of the Negro Burns at Boston. Now, in Concord, he was an eager listener to John Brown at the Town Hall. Brown, he thought, told his story with surpassing simplicity and sense, impressing his audience by his courage and his religious earnestness. Alcott observed with approval that the best Concord people were present to hear Brown, and contributed to his plans without asking particulars. When Brown had been hanged, and when a meeting had been called in Concord to honor the martyr's courageous death, Alcott joined Emerson and Thoreau, who had chiefly arranged for the meeting, in speaking at the occasion, and Louisa sent some commemorative verses to Garrison's *Liberator*. He agreed early with Emerson that the war must issue in freeing the slaves. And Louisa's experience as a nurse in a Union hospital in Washington, D. C., where she was seriously ill, was a matter of pride and deepest concern to all the Alcotts.

Again, as in his earlier Concord residences, Alcott spent the warm seasons in his garden and orchard, and these occupied both his time and his affections; but in the idle days and the long nights of winter he was busying himself, as in the years of his first acquaintance with Emerson, with his writing. It had been a decade and more since he had last spoken with his friend about "Psyche," which was now filed away among what Alcott called his Transcripts. Now, however, he was working on his "Book of Men and Opinions," and on some papers on the "Country Man in His Garden." Emerson, he feared, doubted, as usual, that they were good, but was persuaded to come and hear some pages read. Alcott diffidently read the sketches of Goethe, Carlyle, and Thoreau, and pleased himself with fancying that his critic found them better than he had expected. Of the paper on himself, which Alcott entitled the "Rhapso- dist," Emerson accepted some of the traits, but disclaimed the praise, said that it might be read in private circles, but must not appear in print, though Fields, who had succeeded Lowell as editor of the *Atlantic,* wished it for his pages. Though Emerson had once long ago urged Alcott to write as a way to fulfill his mission in the world, he now still held to the view he had expressed when he had advised that "Psyche" be not published. Alcott's whim for writing, he had long assured himself, was a false instinct, like Goethe's for sculpture, over which both of them had lost much good time. But he did not urge his conviction; instead, he sug- gested that Alcott publish his "Inventory of the Mind," which, he said, should have a place in the *Atlantic* as a paper on the science of classification, and good for the naturalist and the metaphysician. Though Alcott agreed, he wished to give it a more thorough consideration, and so he put it away—as, long ago, he had put "Psyche" away lest it come misshapen into the world.

After Fruitlands had failed, it had been one of Alcott's hopes to teach in Concord, and one of his bitter disappoint- ments that even the little primary school across from Emer- son's had been denied him. Now, in the second year after his return from Walpole, and quite unsolicited by him, he was honored by being made superintendent of the Concord public schools. The position was, indeed, mainly an honorary one (at $100 a year!), but it was clearly a local recognition, and gave him such happiness as he had not had in many years. He walked from school to school, talked to the pupils (where was there ever a more expert teacher than he?), gave advice to the instructors, and wrote annual reports, one, at least, a national classic of its kind. But he was happiest at the school festivals which he introduced, when all the children of Concord gathered for exercises at the Town Hall. He was in his glory, Louisa said, and like a happy shepherd with a large flock of sportive lambs. For the festival in the first year of the war, Louisa had composed a song, to which there was some objection from those who did not like the inclusion of the names of Wendell Phillips and John Brown. But Emerson would not hear of making changes, and read the verses himself; and then, wrote Louisa in her diary, the choir warbled, and the Alcotts were uplifted in their vain minds.[19]

These Concord days gave Alcott new hope of himself and of the world around him. At home, it was pleasant to take a turn about his grounds, or to work in his orchard or garden and thus unite man and nature. And what pleasure it was to gather the fruits of such labors! in the summer, to eat strawberries and cream at Emerson's with Hawthorne, and Thoreau, and Sanborn; and, in winter, to carry baskets of apples and bottles of cider to his friends. He was glad, too, when friends called, as, one day while he was cutting birches on the hill, Emerson came with Whittier. But within the circle of his own family he found the incidents, the virtues, which idealized his existence. May was grown up now, studying art, and said by her teachers to be of great promise—a tall, blond girl, full of grace and spirit. Louisa, alternately at Boston and at Concord, was leading a busy life of teaching, sewing, writing—bringing home money for the family, and hoping some day to make

a hit with one of her stories. She was full of energy and
humor, and Alcott was as happy as any of the young people
who gathered in his parlor to hear Louisa read her lecture
on "Strong-minded Women," or her parody on Emerson's
"The Sphinx." When she was absorbed in writing her
Moods, sitting in groves of manuscript, and, as May said,
living for immortality, Alcott was pleased and brought his
reddest apples and his hardest cider for her Pegasus to
feed upon. One day late in May, when his apple trees were
in luxuriant blossom, Anna was married to John Pratt.
The parents and guests danced round the bridal pair under
the old elms, and Emerson kissed Anna—an honor, Louisa
thought, that might make even matrimony endurable,
though she really preferred to be a free spinster and paddle
her own canoe. When, three years later, Anna's first boy
arrived, Alcott confronted a fact which he could not encompass for joy, and he walked about his house repeating,
"Anna's boy! yes, yes, Anna's boy." Even artistic Aunt
May condescended to say that the baby was a very nice
thing.[20]

If the Alcotts had once been the "pathetic" family, about
whom Louisa planned to write a story some day, they were
a very happy family now. Alcott himself, if not quite as
poor as poverty, was, however, now almost as serene as
heaven. That was the great treasure which the years had
brought him.

IV

His own philosophy, Emerson thought, consisted of only
a few laws: first, *Identity,* whence comes the fact that meta-
physical faculties and facts are the transcendency of physical; and, secondly, *Flowing,* or transition, or shooting the
gulf, the perpetual striving to ascend to a higher platform,
the same thing in new and higher form. His basic prin-

ciples of conduct, moreover, were few: abandon yourself to the leading, when the Master comes, for such is the sum of wisdom and duty; shake off from your shoes the dust of Europe and Asia, the rotten religions and personalities of nations; and act from your heart, where the wise temperate guidance is instantly born. And beneath these abstractions, motivating them, giving them life, was the joy which would not let him sit in his chair, which brought him bolt upright to his feet, sent him striding around his room, like a tiger in his cage, and would not permit composure and concentration enough even to set down in words the thought which thrilled him. Was not that joy a certificate of the verity of his principles? What if he never wrote a book or a line? For a moment, the eyes of his eyes were opened, the affirmative experience remained and consoled through all suffering.[21]

Such was the ecstasy, such were the beatitudes. But there were dull days, too, and irritations, and endless commonplaces. Today, carpets; yesterday, the aunts; the day before, the funeral of poor S.; and every day, the remembrance in the library of the rope of work which he must spin. In this way was his life dragged down and confuted. He tried to listen to the hymn of the gods, and must needs hear this perpetual *cock-a-doodle-doo,* and *ke-tar-kut,* right under his library windows. They, the gods, ought to respect a life, one should think, whose objects were their own. But steadily they threw mud and eggs at their worshipers, rolled them in the dirt, and jumped on them.

A good many things happened in the scholar's year to spoil his days and deprive him of the freedom friendly to a spontaneous flow of thought. The furnace smoked, the roof leaked, the plaster came off the ceiling, the "new man" had to be broken in, the mare went lame, the fruit crop was poor this year, the rain spoiled the hay in the

heater-piece.   In climbing down Mt. Wachusett, he
sprained his ankle.   "A splint," said Dr. B., "and absolute
rest."   "Rest, yes," said Dr. R., "but no splint."   And at
Concord, Dr. Bartlett: "Go and walk, or you never will."
Clear, wasn't it?   The crutch made his hand numb, and he
could not write.   He walked with a cane, thought that he
looked seventy, feared that he had come to talk like seventy.
Then his door was beset with beggars every day, the Sar-
dinians and Sicilians, who could not argue the question of
labor and mendicity because they did not speak a word of
English.   There were agents, too—a chipping lady from
the Cape, who had three blind sisters, and he knew not how
many dumb ones, and she had been advised to put them
in the poorhouse.   No, not she.   As long as she had health,
she would go about and sell these books for them, which
he was to buy, and she tossed her head, and expected his
praise and tears for her heroic resolution, though he had a
puzzled feeling that, if there was a sacrifice anywhere, it
was in him, if he should buy her books.   He was sure that
he was little inclined to toss *his* head.

In the midst of such wasted days, he sometimes believed
that he had no new thoughts and that his life was quite
at an end.   That he was growing old he could not deny.
Well, one capital advantage of old age was the absolute
insignificance of a success more or less.   He had gone to
town the other day to read a lecture.   Thirty years ago it
had really been a matter of importance to him whether it
was good and effective.   Now it was of no importance to
him.   It was long ago fixed what he could and what he
could not do.   Furthermore, when he had reached the end
of his fifty-seventh year, he was easier in his mind than
before.   He could never give much reality to evil or pain.
But now when Lidian asked whether the tumor on his
shoulder might not be a cancer, he could say, What if it is?

Nevertheless, a few years later, he thought it perhaps a little strange that there was no vogue to commit hari-kari at sixty. Nature, as Ellery said, is so insulting in her hints and notices; does not pull you by your sleeve, but pulls out your teeth, tears off your hair in patches, steals your eyesight, twists your face into an ugly mask; in short, puts all contumelies upon you, without in the least abating your zeal to make a good appearance. And all this at the same time that she is molding the new figures around you into wonderful beauty, which, of course, is only making your plight worse.

Perhaps, in the matter of old age, the world could be more appropriately constructed, so that after sixty a certain mist or dimness, a sort of autumnal haze, would settle on the figure, veiling especially all decays. Gradually, year by year, the outline would become indistinct, and the halo gayer and brighter. At last, there would be only left a sense of presence, and the virtue of personality, as if Gyges never turned his ring again. Such revisions would be an immense social convenience.[22]

In the meantime, happiness nevertheless required a few companions of intelligence, probity, and grace with whom one could wear out one's life. As for himself, Emerson thought that he was his own man more than most men, could better endure and enjoy solitude more than most, yet a few persons were necessary to his welfare, to give flesh to what were else mere thoughts. Ellery he continued to find, from month to month, and from year to year, an incomparable companion, lively, witty, inexhaustible. It would be too much to say that he might have learned to treat the Platonic world as cloudland had he not known Alcott, yet he could say that Alcott made that world as solid as Massachusetts to him. And Thoreau gave him, in flesh and blood and pertinacious Saxon belief, his own ethics.

Thoreau was far more real, and practically more obeying
them, than he, and fortified his memory at all times with
an affirmative experience which refused to be set aside.

He was taking a good many walks with Henry in these
years—to Acton, to Sawmill Brook, to Conatum, to Goose
Pond, to the Cliffs, to the Estabrook country, to Everett's
pasture, to Walden. Henry would come with a music book
under his arm, to press flowers in; with telescope in his
pocket to see the birds, and miscroscope to count stamens;
with a diary, jackknife, and twine; in stout shoes, and strong
grey trousers, ready to brave the shrub-oaks and smilax,
and to climb the tree for a hawk's nest. He was more and
more preoccupied with the identification and classification
of the plant life of Concord. By Everett's spring he pointed
out to Emerson *Saxifraga pennsylvanica, Chrysoplenium
oppositifolium, Stellaria, Cerastium;* up the Assabet they
found the *Azalea nudiflora* in full bloom, the *Viola Muhlen-
bergi,* the *Ranunculus recurvatus.* The flora of Massachusetts, Henry said, embraced almost all the important plants
of America. He thought, too, that nothing could be hoped
from you if this bit of mold under your feet was not sweeter
to you to eat than any other in this world, or in any world.
If only Henry had a little ambition in his mixture, Emerson
reflected, he might be the leader of American engineers; but
lacking ambition, he was captain of huckleberry parties.
Besides, he often seemed stubborn and implacable; always
manly and wise, but rarely sweet. It was difficult to hold
intercourse with his mind. Still, it was a great convenience
to know one who knew what was on the land, who could
go wherever woods and waters were, who could take you
to the watery haunts of the elder gods and show you the
mists rising. No doubt Henry had chosen wisely to be the
bachelor of thought and nature that he was.[23]

Of Ellery, Emerson thought that he had more poetic

temperament than any other in America, though he had not the artistic executive power of completing a design. His poetry was like the artless warbling of the vireo, which whistles prettily all day and all summer in the elm, but never rounds a tune. It was wanting in clear statement, and made only a hazy, indefinite impression. Still, it was an autumnal air, and like the smell of the herb Life Ever-lasting.[24]

But Ellery was a veteran walker, and found wonders of color and landscape everywhere. The Ellery who went on walks was a rare and rich compound of gods and dwarfs, and the best of humanity, a perpetual holiday. Could any-one, Emerson had wondered, bring home the summits of Wachusett and Monadnoc, the juniper fields of Lincoln, and the sedge and reeds of Flint's Pond, or the savage woods beyond Nut Brook toward White Pond? Well, Ellery could, and did.

Their lives had been spun together in these numberless walks through the years, and yet each new expedition yielded a cornucopia of golden joys. In the autumn, on the Old Marlboro Road, they saw heaps of yellow apples in every enclosure, whole orchards ungathered, and in the Grecian piazzas of the houses, a profusion of pumpkins ripening between the columns. They walked over hill and dale, and on a mild November day saw the fields in every direction covered with cobwebs, on which the wake of the setting sun appeared as on water. On a December afternoon they made a new discovery, the reflections of trees in the ice. There were snowflakes on the ice, too, perfect rowels; beautiful groups of icicles all along the eastern shore of Flint's Pond, the union of the flowing with the fixed. How many days could Methuselah go abroad and see somewhat new?

It was the summer days, he and Ellery sometimes thought, that were the best in the year. When Flint's Pond

was in its summer glory, the chestnuts in flower, and thun-
dertops in the sky, the whole picture was a study of all
the secrets of landscape. The woods were then at their best,
flecked with spots of pure sunshine everywhere—paths for
Una and her lamb. It was delicious to live. One must
come to see such a sight, Ellery said; it could never be
imagined. Yet Ellery believed nature less interesting than
man, though Thoreau had said that nature was more so,
and persons less. Emerson told Ellery that he would always
have nature combined with man. Life, he thought, was
ecstatical, and men radiate joy and honor and gloom on the
days and landscapes they converse with. But he remembered
that in his youth they who had spoken to him of nature
were religious, and made it so, and made it deep.

As for Alcott, he never had been a great walker, and
now, since he was so absorbed in his garden and orchard,
he rarely went walking with Emerson, even to Walden,
though the two occasionally took a turn around the triangle
that lay along the Great Road between their houses. But
Emerson regarded him as an inestimable companion, nevertheless. He told Alcott that he should describe him as a
man with a divination or good instinct for the quality and
character of wholes; as a man who looked at things in a
little larger angle than most other persons; and as one
who had a certain power of transition from thought to
thought, as by secret passages, which it would tax the
celerity and subtlety of good metaphysicians to follow. In
Emerson's private reflections, the obscurity of Alcott was a
constant wonder. He himself had found Alcott as good as
a lens or mirror, a beautiful susceptibility, every impression
on which was not to be reasoned against, or derided, but
to be accounted for, and until accounted for, registered as
an indisputable addition to our catalogue of natural facts.
There were defects in the lens, and errors of refraction and

position to be allowed for, and it needed one acquainted with the lens by frequent use to make these allowances; but it was, for Emerson, the best instrument he had ever met with.[25]

These were Emerson's most intimate friends. They were the reasonable creatures to whom he needed to talk, to keep his sanity, and to refresh the resources with which to meet the world. It was they who largely sustained him, they and solitude and nature. He was controlled, he knew, by powers deeper than could be told, powers which belonged to the immensities and eternities, and reached down to that depth where society itself originates, and where he, the private individual, was lost in his source. But even in these vast and sky-vaulted fields in which he walked alone, he was cheered and renewed by the simplest objects: the beautiful color of the apple heaps, more lively and varied than the orange—balls of scarlet fire; what gaiety and depth they gave to drab Massachusetts! Nor did age dull these pleasures. The world, for him, wore well. The autumn afternoons and well-marbled landscapes of green and gold and sunset, and steel-blue river, and smoke-blue New Hampshire mountains, remained as perfect penciling as ever.

What he studied in nature, of course, was always found to be the study of man, and it was that fact which gave edge to his inquiry, for, if an independency and foreignness in nature could be shown, he was sure that he should never care for it more. And yet, how the landscape mocked the weakness of man—the landscape so vast, beautiful, complete, and alive, and man capable only of dibbling and stepping about and dotting it a little! There was something finer in earth and sky, it seemed to him, than his senses could appreciate, something that escaped him, and yet was only just beyond his reach. He had asked the question long ago: What is it that Nature would say?

Yes, and this gulf between our seeing and our doing was a symbol of that between faith and experience.[26]

For him, at least, the first source of inspiration was in solitary converse with nature. There, in nature, he found sweet and dreadful words never uttered in libraries.

Ah, the spring days, and summer dawns, and October woods!

V

But beyond these long, level plains lay precipices and ravines. In spite of the war, the private lives and the friendship of Alcott and Emerson had been moving smoothly enough; now, however, certain situations arose which brought great changes of which both became sharply aware.

There was, for one thing, the growing consciousness in Alcott's mind of the importance to him of what he called personality. It was, of course, a thought which had passed through his mind when he had first intimately spoken with Emerson on that eventful first visit to Concord now so many years ago. But in the enthusiasm of enjoying such a multitude of views in common, because of his great admiration for Emerson, and because of the dominance of Emerson's character and fame, Alcott had permitted this thought to lie quiescent, though it had perhaps never left his mind. Was it purely a coincidence, then, that the friends should be discussing the subject in Emerson's study late into the February night, while Elizabeth lay fatally ill, two days before her death?

The problem took form for Alcott in a number of ways. It occurred to him in his library one rainy and snowy November night, as he thumbed through the pages of Emerson's books, that these volumes were very good—might, indeed, form an adequate hope for a church if they did not lack some kind of personal unity, if they were not so impersonal. Something of the kind he had thought as he had read *English Traits;* that the sketches of men there were very fine in profile, though the portraits and personalities were not so fine. Some immediate coloring was lacking, some solvent of common sense in the sentiments, an alchemy subtler than even Emerson's imagination could compass and command, and so left the pictures incomplete, the parts marvelously individual, but the personality some-where at fault, nevertheless, and the whole but a sketch un-finished. He had even ventured to tell Emerson that his essay on "Worship" gave the worshipful temperament, but not the worship. In his own diary he had admitted, in spite of his love for Emerson, that no simple, devout soul, man or maid, would find there what he sought.[27]

If Alcott approached this question with some hesitation and circumlocution, Emerson looked at it with more assur-ance and directness. He was impatient with those who pro-fessed to be spiritualists and yet in their every word on Deity confessed to a stiff and indigent anthropomorphism. The demarcations which some regarded as essential to their religious convictions he had found resolved thirty years ago in Xenophanes and Parmenides and now in his Oriental readings, some of which he had only recently put to verse.

> They reckon ill who leave me out;
> When me they fly, I am the wings;
> I am the doubter and the doubt,
> And I the hymn the Brahmin sings.

Alcott's thesis of personality was not to him a satisfactory use of words. His reply to Alcott was that we speak daily of a government of power used to personal ends. He saw a profound need of distinguishing the First Cause as superpersonal. It deluges us with power, indeed; we are filled with it, but there are skies of immensity between us and it.[28]

Alcott's true strength, however, lay in the emphasis which he gave to partnership against the doctrine of fate. In Alcott's view, there was no passive reception: the receiver, to receive, must play the God also. Emerson recognized the point as in part opposing what he himself had accepted from Plotinus and the Quakers:

> The passive Master lent his hand
> To the vast soul that o'er him planned.

And there the difference lay, waiting such change or growth as time might bring.

With Ellery, too, there were difficulties—both for Emerson and for Alcott. He was unhappy in his marriage, was trying unsuccessfully to establish himself as a lecturer, was sometimes near despair, and feared that whatever pleased him God would not permit. He urged Emerson to help him with the managers of country lyceums and complained that now that his friend was rich, successful, and caressed, he could not expect aid from him. Ah, if Emerson could have but an hour's experience of the deep and dreadful gulf that was his life! Sometimes he thought that his friendship with Emerson was coming to an end, now that Emerson was so conservative and fortunate. With Alcott, though he had once spoken of him as no icicle (like the Jameses), but warm and sweet, a perfect prince and jewel of a man, he quarreled outright. Alcott had been writing to David Wasson regarding his sonnets, saying that they reminded him of Shakespeare's more than any modern sonnets. Channing, having read the note, coolly advised Alcott to burn it; and then, Alcott suggesting that he find the door forthwith, Channing left and did not return. Now Alcott caught no more than a glimpse of him as he passed the house once

in a long while. He avoided Alcott's door—tried to avoid
his glance when they met in the streets. It seemed to
Alcott that Ellery, alas, was a capricious man![29]

But even before this unhappy incident of Alcott's with
Channing, there had been a much more serious break—the
death of Henry. In mid-December Alcott had called on
him when Henry had just returned from lecturing at
Waterbury, where he had spoken with a severe cold. Two
weeks later, when Alcott came again (to bring apples and
cider!), Henry was feeble and failing. He was talkative,
however, in whispers, and still interested in books and men,
in the civil troubles especially, and spoke impatiently of
what he called the temporizing of the administration. In
the first week in May he was dead. Alcott called at the
Thoreau house, and listened to Henry's mother as she told
about his last moments. His sister, Sophia, was there, too,
and lifted the cloth for Alcott to see Henry's face. He
looked as when he had last seen him, Alcott reflected—only
a tinge of paler hue. He had been forty-four years last
July.

Alcott stooped over and kissed the brow upon which
the damps and sweat of death now lay. Alcott himself was
sixty-two, grey, and venerable.

As Emerson walked in his woods about Walden, there,
before him in the fragrant pines, was Henry—erect, calm,
and self-subsistent.[30]

Then, two years later, Hawthorne died, and was buried
in Sleepy Hollow in a pomp of May sunshine, apple blossoms, and gentle winds. All was so bright that pain or
mourning was hardly suggested, but it seemed, rather, a
happy meeting.

But Emerson, who with Alcott was among the pall-
bearers, thought that there was a tragic element in the event
nevertheless. Hawthorne, he supposed, could no longer

endure his solitude, and had died of it. Hawthorne was a greater man than any of his works betrayed, it seemed to Emerson, and he had thought that there was still a great deal of work in him; and so his death was a surprise and disappointment. Moreover, he had felt sure of Hawthorne in his neighborhood, felt that he would one day fulfill the friendship that had begun twenty years ago in their memorable walk to Harvard village and the Shakers. But Hawthorne was so silent, and Emerson feared that he himself talked too much, feared that he would offend. One day when Emerson met him on the top of his hill, in the woods back of his house, Hawthorne paced the path despondingly. This path, he said, would be the only remembrance of him to remain.

Now the friendship which Emerson had wished could no longer be. It appeared that he had waited too long.[31]

When Margaret had died in a storm at sea, with her husband and child, in the year after his second return from England, Emerson had felt that he must hurry now to his work, admonished that he had few days left. Then, during Henry's illness, he had observed that, as he lived longer, it seemed that his company were picked out to die first, and that he was living on in a lessening minority.

It was as Alcott said: the fair figures of their village were one by one fading from sight. Emerson and he were almost alone.

FANCY DEPARTS

THE IMPORT OF THESE harbingers was for Emerson unmistakable. Margaret's death was of course accidental, though when rescue was offered and seemed possible she had chosen to remain on shipboard and die with her husband and child. But Hawthorne was a year younger than Emerson, and Henry was his junior by fourteen years.

Though Alcott thought that Emerson retained the countenance of youth, and the members of his own family regarded him as looking healthy, full of life, and young in spirit, he himself calmly recognized that his powers had begun to fail. Edward, now a youth of twenty-two, was startled to make the discovery. He had met his father in New York as the latter was departing for another winter tour of lecturing in the West. They had sat before a fireplace in their hotel, and Emerson had read some of his recent verses.[1]

No more!

No farther shoot
Thy broad ambitious branches, and thy root.
Fancy departs: no more invent;
Contract thy firmament. . . .

Emerson was, in short, losing some of his zest for the tumult which he once so eagerly entered. Now, it seemed to him, it was tedious, the squalor and obstructions of travel of these endless trips, these numberless lectures, this dragging of a decorous old gentleman out of his home to a juvenile career. It was tantamount to betting him that for fifty dollars a day he would not leave his library and wade and ride and run and suffer all manner of indignities, and stand up an hour each night reading in a hall—it was tantamount to that and his acceptance of the bet and winning $900 in the season. He had not meant to travel westward again, and yet old promises and the need of earning money still drew him into the bitter cold, still farther now, into Kansas and Minnesota, into the young country which was America in the raw, and which needed the best sunshine in winter to make it endurable. The performance of the settlers, he knew, was wonderful, and yet, when he saw, in this rough yeomanly lair of the giants, some Eastern woman, born to be delicate and petted, the situation was no less than pathetic. People were kind to him, it was true, but in all this swarming country he hardly ever saw anybody whom he had seen before. It seemed to him now that, for scholars at least, Landor was right when he wrote: "Who would live in a new country when he can live in an old one?"[2]

He would find himself, he thought, more at home before Eastern audiences, and to them he would like to limit his addresses. Still, when Harvard invited him to deliver a series of lectures for advanced students, he came home from his first lecture in despondency. He had joined, he feared, the dim choir of bards who had been. Here were eighteen lectures, he wrote to Carlyle, each to be read sixteen miles from his house, to go and to come, the same work and journey twice each week. A second year, he had thought, and the task would be less and the pleasure greater; but the second year came and went, without, however, a greater feeling of success. He was sure that he had an abundance of good readings and some good writing for the thirty students in his class, though in his haste and confusion these things were always misplaced or spoiled. He hoped that the ruin of no young man's soul would, here or hereafter, be charged to him for having wasted the student's time or confused his reason. At any rate, the college course he regarded as a doleful ordeal which gave him anxiety and made him fatigued.[3]

Was it rest that he needed? He consented to a westward journey to California in the private car of his good friend John M. Forbes, whose son William had married Edith. Edith would not permit her father to say no. Hence, for the first time, he spanned the entire country. He saw, on the great plains, multitudes of antelopes, hares, gophers, elks; but, though he passed through the buffalo region, was disappointed in seeing none. At every railroad station there were Indians, the squaws and papooses begging, and the "bucks," as he thought them perhaps wickedly called, lounging. He paid a visit to Salt Lake City, and called on Brigham Young, then just seventy years old, who received him with courtesy. Young was a strong-built, self-possessed, and sufficient man, with plain manners, Emerson thought, and full of Franklinian good sense. In California, it seemed to Emerson, the chief attraction and superiority was in its days. It had better days, and more of them, than any other country. It was rich, too, in trees and endless flowers, and made New England seem starved in comparison, though over this new garden lay an awe and terror—all empty as yet of any adequate people. In San Francisco, he visited Chinatown, saw the Chinese shops—butcher and vegetable and flower shops, with all the Chinamen dressed in blue robes and wearing queues reaching almost to their feet. He lectured in Oakland and San Francisco, and was amused by the report in a San Francisco paper that his lecture on "Immortality" had been called an elegant tribute to the creative genius of the Great First Cause. In brief, he enjoyed his journey and came home greatly refreshed.[4]

And then, in the last week of July in the following summer, his house burned. He had been awakened, on a rainy morning, somewhat after daybreak, by the crackling of fire in the walls of his bedroom. A few hours later, drenched and exhausted, he saw that his house was almost totally destroyed, the walls of the lower floor alone still standing. It was, he tried to assure himself, ridiculous that a fire should make an old scholar sick; but it was useless to conceal that the exposure of that morning, and the necessities of the following days which had kept him a large part of the time in the blaze of the sun, had for the present, at least, completely demoralized him.

Alcott came to see him at the Old Manse, where the family had been invited by Emerson's cousin. Alcott came bringing copies of *The History of the First Church,* by Emerson's father, and Rantoul's "Nineteenth of April Oration," which Emerson was not sure had been saved, though most of his library escaped from the flames. The friends walked about the grounds where old Dr. Ripley had lived so many years, along the river, and to the monument. They explored the house together, too, and climbed into the attic, still primitive, and examined the inscriptions of Emerson's father and others on the walls of the Prophet's Chamber. The spinning wheels in the attic reminded Alcott of his mother's and sisters' wheels and of their spinning. It was fortunate, Alcott reflected, that Emerson could come here, to the house which his own grandfather had built, and where he himself had written so much of *Nature* thirty-seven years ago.[5]

It was apparent, however, that the experience of the fire had been a rude shock from which Emerson did not seem to recover. So another vacation was proposed, and he was persuaded to visit once more England, France, Italy, and, for the first time, Egypt, where, he said, he wished to see the tomb of "him who sleeps at Philae." His daughter

Ellen accompanied him—Ellen, who was so capable, and in whose hands he gladly placed himself, and upon whom he more and more relied. In Europe, many doors were now open to him, and he discovered the convenience of having a name—that it served as well as having a good coat. At Chelsea, he saw Carlyle again. Carlyle had gazed at him a long time, and then opened his arms and embraced him. He was glad to see Emerson in the flesh once more, he said. Then, as twenty-five years ago, there was a steady outpouring for two or three hours on persons, events, and opinions. Carlyle still played his old game of satire on men and things generally. When, curious to know Carlyle's reaction to the men and authors whom Emerson himself now admired, Emerson spoke of his favorites, he got them all back again, of course, in Carlyle's Scottish speech and wit, with large deduction of size. In spite of his seventy-seven years, Carlyle's memory was good, and he was as strong in person and manners as ever, only he had become so aged looking. Jane had been dead six years.[6]

The excursion to Egypt provided Emerson the greatest novelty. At Alexandria he marveled at the colossal temples. scattered over hundreds of miles, all the more wonderful because no creature remained to give hint of the men who made them. He wondered, too, at the profusion of buildings and sculptures—at statues by the fifties and hundreds. On the Nile, day after day and week after week of unbroken sunshine, the clouds in sky merely for ornament and never bringing rain. The Nile itself had the appearance of a long lake whose end the boat was always fast approaching but whose shores always separated into new lakes. The cultivated land was a mere green ribbon on either shore of the river, beyond which lay rocky mountains or desert sands. At the water's edge were palm groves; round about, innumerable birds—the ibis, the penguin, with vast flights of ducks and geese, and flocks of little birds who flew in rolling globes and whirled around and around and returned again every minute. Cairo was a mob of all colors and all costumes and of no costume at all which crowded the streets and lanes of the aged city. It made one think that one was dreaming, and dreaming a wild rather than a pleasant dream. Turk, Copt, Arab, Nubian, Italian, German, English, and American filled the narrow and unpaved streets and lanes.[7]

Once Emerson had called travel a fool's paradise. Now, back again in Europe, he was aware of its pleasures. When he arrived in a new city, Rome, or Florence, or Paris, he had a feeling of free adventure: he had no duties, nobody knew him, nobody claimed him; he was like a boy again in Boston on his first visit to the Common on election day. Here he was, alone in these huge old cities, with all their wonders, architecture, gardens, ornaments, galleries—all of which had never cost him so much as a thought. For the first time in years he wakened master of the bright days, in a bright world, without a claim on him. Household cares he had none. He took dinner, lunch, or supper where and when he would. Cheap cabs waited for him at every corner, guides at every door; sumptuous goods and attractive merchandise, unknown hitherto, solicited his eyes. His health mended every day. Every word spoken to him was a wonderful riddle which it was a pleasure to solve. Every experience of the day seemed important and furnished conversation for him—for him who was so silent at home.

In Concord once more, he felt well enough to deliver an occasional lecture. One invitation to speak he especially could not refuse. It was an auspicious sign, he thought, when the University of Virginia sent to Massachusetts for a commencement speaker. Certainly he, who had been so ardent in the Northern cause, could not deny this gesture of reconciliation.[8]

He had not been in the South since, in the uncertain days of his youth, he had strolled on the beach in Florida, driving green oranges over the sand with a stick, and wondering whether he should live to use the sermons he was writing. It was therefore another adventure when he and Ellen, in the last week in June, journeyed southward to Charlottesville. Everywhere trains were filled with people on their way to the great Centennial Exhibition at Philadelphia, men in long black coats and tall silk hats, and women in ruffles and bustles and trailing gowns. Everywhere people were talking about General Custer, and the annihilation of his troops by the Sioux. As Emerson's train moved through Virginia, he was surrounded by novel and interesting scenes. Here almost every foot had been trod by the opposing armies, vestiges of the struggles still remaining: villages not yet recovered, cemeteries with rows upon rows of mounds. Everywhere were Negroes, especially in the cities, where the black children ran and shouted beside the train, where dusky drivers of hacks and carriages offered their services, and where venders of food, carrying on their heads platters of fried chicken and sandwiches and fruit, walked the station platforms and cried their wares. The country was no less interesting, with its wooded hills, its huts and cabins, its large estates, and its beautiful drooping willows.

It was a warm June night; and gaslighted Public Hall, in which Emerson was to lecture, was filled to overflowing with the sons and daughters of the Sunny South, for at commencement, not only parents and brothers, but sisters and sweethearts were invited to the festivities, the latter not chiefly to listen to the commencement address, but to join in the endless dancing of the "German" which was then in vogue, and to promenade under the Chinese lanterns along the Arcades and on the moonlit lawn. Now, in the breathless air of the hall, there was a fluttering of hundreds of fans, the whispering of young men and their sweethearts, the stir and hum and general commotion of an audience waiting for the exercises to begin. The band played, the chaplain offered a prayer, and the speaker was introduced.

There, behind the speaker's stand, a kerosene lamp beside his manuscript, stood Emerson, braving the heat in black dresscoat, waistcoat, high collar and stock. His hair, once a vigorous brown, was now grey, only thin strands covering the top of his head. The eyes, which were once so piercing, were shaded by spectacles and were kept close to his manuscript. When he began to read, his voice was scarcely audible beyond a half-dozen rows, and young Virginia, certain that it could not hear, returned to those pleasant diversions which had been interrupted when the band began to play.

In the eyes of the world—the same world which, when Alcott was forty-eight, had seen only his grey hair and apparent failure—it was evident that Emerson was now merely an elderly gentleman, spectacled and somewhat stoop-shouldered, whom time and life had really quite passed by.

II

Strangely enough, while Emerson's fortunes, in one sense of the word, were thus in their decline, Alcott's were in their ascendancy. Alcott was enjoying a perhaps greater bodily vigor than formerly, and the recognition and success for which he had waited so many years were coming at last.

He was experiencing, for one thing, a renewed pleasure and hope in his writing. At this long time afterward, Emerson's criticism of "Psyche" seemed a frank criticism of a friend, kind and just. It was fortunate that Emerson had spoken when he did, and thus withheld the manuscript from the press, though the experience had been disheartening at the time and made impossible any writing beyond that in the diary. His style in those days, it seemed to Alcott now, had been vicious in the extreme. He was offended even by the "Introduction" to the *Conversations,* which Emerson had thought well of and praised at the time. It was not until after the Fruitlands adventure that he had come to the style with which he could be somewhat content.

He had begun his new writing career modestly enough— with the private publication of his pages on Emerson in a little book, the printing and binding and ornamentation of which he could not but regard as perfect. It was a delightful May day, outdoors and within his thoughts, when he penned a note to Mrs. Emerson and brought her his little book for her husband's birthday. Emerson himself came, a few days later, to express his pleasure with the gift and to praise the binding, the printing, and the style. As for the text, that was such a Persian superlative that he had to shade his eyes as if to accept only a part of the meaning. He scarcely knew whether it gave him more pleasure or more pain, though he admired the generous sentiment and the wish to convey good will.[9]

Then with the publication of *Tablets,* and presently the request for a second printing, Alcott was encouraged anew. Even the winter months seemed springlike, and he had whole days of delight over his new manuscript, and delicious slumbers afterwards, much as in the year when he had been building Emerson's summerhouse. When *Concord Days* had gone into a third edition, and the last copies nearly sold, he could, in the booksellers' sense, at any rate, regard his writing a success. He took pleasure now in looking at his books as they stood in a row on his study table. When he picked up *Concord Days,* he was tempted to read page after page and run it through to the last. Editors, he thought, might quote less suggestive passages from popular writers like Henry Ward Beecher or Robert Collyer. Some of his own pages even seemed comparable to Emerson's, and he fancied them as suggestive and as quotable.

Still, when he had met Emerson at the post office, and Emerson had encouraged him to put to paper his thoughts on immortality, Alcott was reluctant to speak about his writing. He might have told Emerson that his notes would find place in the new volume which he would call *Table Talk;* but he hesitated to speak to Emerson about his writing, or to show him any of it, because his friend was so consummate in his critical judgment, and so exacting. Besides, he had the best of reasons for believing that his style and habit of thought suffered in writing. Perhaps Emerson undervalued his style in writing as much as he overestimated it in conversation. Yet, though Emerson had no peer with his pen, would it be too much to say that he himself had none with his tongue?[10]

The Alcott fortunes were now looking up, too, in quite another quarter. In speaking of children, Alcott had once told Emerson that in his opinion a son translated the privacy of a family to the public; daughters, in fact, could not do it. But that, of course, was before Louisa had written *Little Women* and had at last made the hit which was always her ambition. She had not enjoyed writing the book— never liked girls anyway, or knew many, except her sisters— and she thought her chapters dull, though they were simple and true, and the incidents for the most part really as she and her sisters had lived them. But it had been gratifying to provide her mother with many comforts, and, finally, to pay all the family debts, even the outlawed ones. At twenty she had resolved to make the family independent; at forty she had done so. It had cost her her health, perhaps, but she was still alive—alive and amused when city reporters came to Concord and sat on the stone wall beside the yard and took notes of what she said, or artists sketched her as she picked pears in her father's garden. If anybody thought fame was a blessing, let 'em try it![11]

It was, however, in his conversations, which Emerson had often praised so highly, that Alcott was to attain fame and such financial success as was to be his lot. After his first visit to St. Louis, it is true, he had been glad to leave the slovenly West, had thought how purely Eastern he was. But after he had really become acquainted with the St. Louis group, with Harris, and Brockmeyer, and Kroeger, and the rest of the Hegelians, had seen what profound thought Harris had been able to elicit in his *Journal of Speculative Philosophy,* and had discovered how refreshingly these Westerners set aside deference to custom, and tradition, and authority, he was willing to grant that the West had a formidable attraction. Though Emerson declined to accompany him for the course of conversations in the West which they had discussed, the way was now fairly open to himself, he was sure, to sow, if not to reap, the first fruits of this new country. Perhaps, if Emerson chose to deliver his Cambridge lectures, Providence was preferring to divide labors, assigning one to the East and its university, and sending the other to the broader and fresher fields of the West.

Invited as he now was into the best homes and the most active intellectual circles in the West, Alcott could not but feel that his conversations were becoming something of a triumph. And yet, when he returned to Concord and spoke of his success, Emerson would not, it appeared, take his report without question. Even though he knew that he was tempted to paint *en rose,* names, nevertheless, had their significance. When he could refer to the Round Table, the Plato Club, the Friends in Council, the Philosophical Society, and the *Journal of Speculative Philosophy,* there must needs arise before the imagination a culture and society to pique curiosity and invite inquiries about that world at the West.[12] Emerson himself, he thought, could not have met these people under the best advantages. At any rate, Alcott assured himself, he returned from each Western trip with hopeful and happy memories of the people whom he had met. He congratulated himself, too, on such an opportunity for learning the spirit and manners of the West as was permitted to few of his contemporaries. He could hardly conceive of being received and entertained with hospitalities more cordial and satisfactory. Life in Concord seemed a little tame after the closer fellowships which he had experienced in the West. Even his evenings with Emerson, by contrast, were somewhat disappointing.

That his relations with Emerson were not now what they had been, was very clear to Alcott, though that they were no longer friends was far from his thoughts. On the contrary, he still felt that, next to his marriage, his acquaintance with Emerson was the happiest event of his life. Blot Emerson's home from the landscape and his own would need another tenant than he. He did not see Emerson as often as he desired; he passed his friend's study oftener than he should like, unwilling to interrupt or invade his privacy. Some of their meetings, indeed, were still very pleasant, as when Emerson brought out his diaries and they indulged in early reminiscences of their acquaintance. And something of their first acquaintance appeared to have survived and to have mellowed the fellowship of these later years. Emerson, moreover, still spoke kindly of the conversations—told Alcott that when his theme moved forward so delightfully it was a shame to interrupt the flood, and that there would never be a word to hinder from him. Their friendship was an experience to cherish forever. And yet it seemed to Alcott that he could not expect Emerson to be interested in his new ventures. It was in matters of literature purely and of a personal character that they were in accord and at home. They could hardly expect to continue to surprise one another by new views, as Goethe and Schiller were said to have done. Something of the sort they may have done at the first acquaintance and for some years when their interviews were less frequent and the future had its fresher charms, but not now.

And regrettable though it was, their differences appeared to grow more pronounced, and Alcott became aware of qualities in Emerson that he had not noticed before. Emersons' lecturing, which had first brought them together, Alcott still enjoyed. If not in the popular, at least in the true sense Emerson was an eloquent speaker. While he lived, the Lyceum would manifest the purest devotion taught in their time; when he retired, much of its light and grace would have departed. Another lecturer like Emerson one could not venture to expect. But as an individual, Alcott thought, it might be possible to have with Emerson a deeper sympathy in ideas and social discourse if the drift of his temperament were less dominant. One could wish that he were less positive, more open to persuasion, alike in religious as in political matters, and that his prejudices were not so conspicuous. Emerson questioned and demurred too much; his head was always winning victories over his heart. It was growing more difficult to be familiar with him. If above Boston, he yet led its upper circle, and was becoming popular in an undesirable sense of the word. If he did not like the West, it was perhaps because he was less American than his audience. A Bay State scholar, Emerson was

much of an Old Englander, with something of the air of
blood and culture peculiar to Boston and Cambridge. This
trait was all the more apparent through his sensitive temperament and literary training, and it was this very delicacy
and refinement of exclusiveness that served as native shields
to his genius and made him the man that he was.[13]

There had been no period in Alcott's life when he was
so critical of Emerson, or so assured of his own powers,
a condition perhaps induced by the fact that people listened
to and applauded now what they had ridiculed twenty
years ago. It was not only that he thought that some of his
writing was as suggestive and quotable as Emerson's, as he
had reflected that day in reading his own *Concord Days;*
but his own faculties of discernment were keener. When
he had discussed Hegel in Emerson's study one summer
evening, it had been evident that the Hegelian logic was
strange and unintelligible to them both, though he could
see what Emerson could not—what marvels it could perform
in the hands of a master like Harris, what deep respect it
really merited. When his *Tablets* had been published, he
had thought, too, that the Chicago *Tribune* had spoken truly
of the relation between himself and Emerson: that he was
the teacher to whom Emerson always deferred with rever-
ence; that he bore the relation of master to any younger
living man; that he had been one of the most thoughtful
men in America, more nearly resembling Confucius and
Socrates in his devotion to wisdom than any of his contemporaries; and that in literature Emerson had been to
him as Plato to Socrates, elaborating where he did little
but meditate and converse. The vein of speculation which
Emerson worked was identical with his own. He was an
Emersonian transcendentalist before Emerson was, and if
the latter had been the greater master of literary exposition,

he, Alcott, was the earlier student and teacher of this new philosophy.

It was when he was in such moods, engaged in such trains of thought, that Alcott reassured himself that there were compensations for Emerson's apparent lack of interest in his latest pursuits. Fair and adventurous was the *future*. Perhaps he had always dwelt in it rather than in the present, and perhaps it was in this disparity of outlook that his life and Emerson's had chiefly differed. In this particular, he supposed that he was to remain a youth during his lifetime, and that he must regard those of discreeter views as behind the times.[14]

III

After a rambling talk with Henry late one October night, Emerson remembered only that they had stated over and over again, to sadness, almost, the eternal loneliness. The stuff of tragedy, Emerson had thought, was in the union of two superior persons, and the confidence of each in the other (for long years, out of sight and in sight, and against all appearances) justified at last by victorious proof of probity to gods and men—tragedy consisted in such a union, together with the fatal recognition that this union was only for low and external purposes, like the coopera- tion of a ship's crew, and that no true intellectual identity was after all possible. How insular and pathetically solitary were all the people whom he knew! And he himself, of course, was always ready to recognize what was steady doctrine with him to the end—that though externally men fail to interest us because they seem to be so thoroughly known and exhausted, internally all men have a secret persuasion that, little as they pass for in the world, they are immensely rich in expectancy and power.

The Emerson with whom Alcott now found it so diffi-

cult to share his ideas or even to converse and who had been
so ill equipped to lecture at the University of Virginia, was,
of course, an old man. In conversation with his friends he
was embarrassed because words eluded him even for his
simplest concepts. But within, he did not find wrinkles and
used heart, but unspent youth. Within, he still had his
thoughts, by whatever circuitous route or in whatever words
and images they might come, and to him these thoughts
were still luminous and warm. At seventy he could yet
cite the verses which he had written in the prime of life.

> Spring still makes spring in the mind
>   When sixty years are told:
> Love wakes anew this throbbing heart,
>   And we are never old.
> Over the winter glaciers
>   I see the summer glow,
> And through the wild-piled snowdrift
>   The warm rosebuds below.[15]

When, at sixty-three, Emerson had bid farewell to the
world in "Terminus," the poem which had so startled his
son, he was of course anticipatory, and thinking of his
powers of creation rather than of reflection. Alcott had once
said that his friend's genius lay in his infinite capacity for
hope. It was still hope and cheerfulness which characterized
him in these last years, though writing of any kind was a
heavy task.

Henry he never ceased to admire, but remembered his
fine perceptions, and how, out of doors with him, the poets
had paled like ghosts in the presence of his words. Ellery
still came, though the rural walks were ended, but he came
rarely and complaining of his sad lot, and perhaps unwilling
to be cheered. The conversations of former years with
Alcott, Emerson continued to regard as among the chief

resources of his inspiration. As pure intellect, he had never seen Alcott's equal. Alcott's sight was so clear, commanding the whole ground, and he so perfectly gifted to state adequately what he saw, that he never lost his temper when his glib interlocutors bored him with their dead texts and phrases. It was still a pleasure to watch the perpetual invention and felicity of Alcott's thoughts, and to remark the old fundamental ideas which he had when they first knew each other. The moral benefit of such a mind as Alcott's could not be told. The world faded; men, reputations, politics shriveled; the interests, power, and future of the soul beamed a new dayspring. Faith became sight.[16]

It was true that Emerson had tired of his long excursions to the West, and had difficulty sharing what were still to Alcott novel experiences. It was true, also, that immediately after the war he was disappointed that there did not follow what he had hoped for—true freedom in politics, in religion, in social science, in thought. The energy of the nation seemed to have expended itself in the war, and every interest was as sectional and timorous as before. But he did not despond—welcomed, rather, the criticisms of Renan and Matthew Arnold—even the rude and ignorant things that Ruskin said. If America but mended its faults, it would yet fulfill its proper mission—to make morals practical. In the breaking up of the old traditions of religion, the return to the omnipotence of the moral sentiment should in America be embodied in the laws, in the jurisprudence, in international law, in political economy. America should affirm and establish that in no instance should the guns go in advance of the perfect right.[17]

When Alcott had come to take tea one March afternoon and had left unhappy because he thought Emerson less familiar with his world than he could wish, and feared that Emerson was becoming merely popular, they had talked, among other things, about Plato and Socrates. Emerson had endured Alcott's praises of these men long, and then he had told Alcott that he ought rather to find what was the equivalent for these masters in our own times, what the counterweight and compensation for the modern age. Was it perhaps natural science? It was not merely a remark to provoke conversation. In his diary he observed that Darwin's *Origin of Species* had been published in 1859, but that in 1849 Stallo had already observed that animals are but foetal forms of man. He had great hopes for science. He clung to astronomy, botany, zoology, as read by the severe intellect, and assured himself that he would live and die convinced that he could not go out of the power and Deity which ruled in all his experience, whether sensuous or spiritual. When opened, every secret of geology or chemistry, he was convinced, went to authorize his esthetics. But natural science, without religion, without philosophy, without ethics, was unsouled.[18]

Though Emerson subscribed to Harris's *Journal of Speculative Philosophy,* with Alcott's dallying with the Hegelianism which he confessed he did not understand, Emerson had small sympathy. Dreary to him were the names and numbers of volumes of Hegel and the Hegelians. All that he wanted, Emerson was sure, was to know the one step which the metaphysician had taken. He knew what step Berkeley took, and recognized the same in the Hindu books. Hegel took a second and said that there are two elements, something and nothing, and the two are indispensable at every subsequent step, as well as at the first. Well, that dogma was familiar now, and seemed to have a kind of necessity in it, though poor human nature still felt the paradox. Had Germany any third step of like importance? If so, it scarcely needed an encyclopedia of volumes to tell. As for himself, it was his opinion that the

scholar who abstracted himself with pain to make the analysis of Hegel was less enriched than when the beauty and
depth of any thought by the wayside had commanded his
mind and led to new thought and action; for this process
was healthy, and such thoughts lit up the mind. The scholar
was thus made aware of walls, and also of the way leading
outward and upward, while the other analytic process was
cold and bereaving, and somewhat mean, like spying. In
Emerson's opinion, the metaphysician, dealing, as it were,
with the mathematics of the mind, put himself out of the
way of the inspiration, and lost that which is the miracle
and which creates the worship.

And so, since he could not read Hegel or Schelling, or
find interest in what was told from them, he found it best
to persist in what he called his own idle and easy way, and
wrote down his thoughts, and found presently that there
were congenial persons who liked them, and so he per-
sisted until some kind of outline appeared.[19]

As for Emerson's religious views, some of which were
more and more a matter of concern for Alcott, they were
essentially the views which he had formulated on his return
from Europe on that month-long passage when his ship
had been so badly tossed at sea. He believed in affirmation.
Despair, whining, only betrayed the fact that a man had
been living in the low circle of the senses and the understanding. The sure years must always bring good out of
evil. The charm of the study of religion lay in finding the
agreements and identities in all the religions of men. If
the noblest men of all religions could converse intimately,
two and two, how childish their contrary traditions would
appear! In all men, surely, was this majestic perception
called the moral sentiment, the stupendous mystery with
which we are always familiar, but which passes all explanation. The Universal Mind which imparts this sense of

duty opens the interior world to the humble obeyer, and has done so in all ages. It inspires all, but disdains words and passes understanding. As soon as it is uttered, it is profaned, for it refuses a personality which is instantly imprisoned in human measures.[20]

When he thought of immortality, Emerson confessed that the path of spirit is in silence and hidden from sense. Who knows where or how the soul has existed, before it was incarnated in mortal body? Who knows how or where it thinks and works when it drops its fleshy frame? And what statement of immortality will ever satisfy? The hungry eyes that run through it will close disappointed. As for himself, it seemed to him that immortality was at least equally and perhaps better seen in little than large angles. In a calm and clear state of mind, he had no fears, no prayers, even, but felt that all was well. He had arrived at an enjoyment so pure as to imply and affirm its perfect accord with the nature of things, so that it alone appeared durable, and all mixed or inferior states accidental and temporary.[21]

And if there were no apparent changes in Emerson's political, or philosophical, or religious views in these years before the last infirmities of old age took possession of him, he was, too, still surprised and dazzled by beauty as in the early days of their acquaintance when Alcott had once thought that his friend cared for nothing else. His sympathies were with Critobulus in Xenophon's *Banquet,* who would swear by all the gods that he would choose beauty in preference to the power of the Persian king.[22] Whenever he entered his woodlot at Walden, his spirits rose, and he often spent the whole day there without a remorse of wasting time, still charmed by the bright sunshine on the pond, the shore line, the forest, and the soft lapping sound of the water. Even in the low town of Concord he found an astonishing magnificence when, in October, he saw the colored forests of the Lincoln Hills under the lights and clouds of morning. Then there was the healthy surprise which he experienced when he came out to a sunset sky alone, or when, unexpectedly, he saw the stars. Sometimes, in the street or the drawing room, he thought that there was nothing more ideal in nature than a woman's hair when the wind and the sun played with it, its coils and mass a perpetual mystery and attraction. On a visit to New Hampshire, he was pleased to see the great shadow of Monadnoc lengthen over the plain until it touched the horizon; at Nantasket the long beach was every day renewed with magical shows, with variety of color, with the varied music of the rising and falling water, with multitudes of fishes and birds, of shells and sea-rolled pebbles. And on his study floor, where his grandson played with some trinkets from his desk—where Waldo, too, once had played—he saw all this mystery and charm renewing itself, for there was the boy looking as if he were afraid that these beautiful things would vanish before he had time to see them!

Hovering over all these thoughts remained the old sense of wonder—wonder at what heaven and earth and sea and the forms of men and women were speaking, what fresh perceptions a new day would give of the old problems of his own being and its hidden source—wonder at this sky of law encompassing the world.[23]

IV

Now, when they were both ancients, as Alcott said, they had their greatest difference. They had felt the increasing disparity of their views, of course, before Hawthorne had died, and its recognition had brought a kind of conclusion to many long and unruffled years. But beneath the quiet waters, the crosscurrents had been running from the very beginning of their acquantance, when Alcott had been willing to attribute to differences of association what momentarily had seemed a disparity of idea. Then, when Alcott had visited his friend in Concord in the days when his Boston school had been breaking up, he had returned home disillusioned, he had thought, because Emerson's sympathies had all seemed too intellectual, and Emerson himself an eye rather than a heart. Now once more, but with greater force, and with greater reverberations in the world of men and affairs, their temperaments and their basic ideals asserted themselves. Emerson remained where he had been, in the cool and calm of his Hellenic moorings. But Alcott, who had always really longed for the support of companionship, now unreservedly moved down the current of the Hebraic ideals whose force he had perhaps always felt. Boston was no longer the Boston of Dr. Channing or of Alcott's early manhood, and to these new forces Alcott joined himself, and was at home.

In the year following Hawthorne's death, Alcott had spent the early days of February rereading Emerson's essays —"The Over-Soul," "Spiritual Laws," "Power," "Worship," and "Considerations by the Way." He was troubled again with Emerson's notion of Deity, and disappointed that he found in these essays nothing definitely affirming what was now so much engaging his own thought—the personality of the Supreme Cause. Instead, he found only such phrases as the One, the Law—which only confirmed Alcott in his persuasions that Emerson held to an impersonal or ideal theism, tinged deeply, it pained Alcott to believe, with a pantheistic element.[24] The new lecture on "Character," he told Emerson one night, as they sat in Emerson's study, would not satisfy the religious mind, but needed the complement of personality to make it representative of a universal faith. Then, in the following month, when he heard Emerson read the lecture in Concord, he was more than ever sure that it would not content his generation of Christians. The Law which Emerson idealized so admirably was nevertheless too cold and impersonal to be an object of worship. Several years later, Alcott made the acquaintance of W. H. Channing, like himself a personal theist, with whom, Alcott assured himself, he found more sympathy of thought and purpose than with any other mind of his time. In the convictions engendered by these new kinships and intimacies, he wrote in his diary unequivocally that personality is essential to the idea of spirit and that an impersonal God is an absurdity.[25]

Then, in the year of Emerson's misadventure at the University of Virginia, Alcott had met the Reverend Joseph Cook, the grandiloquent enthusiasms of whose Sunday sermons and Monday lectures were the talk of Boston. Alcott had been attracted by Cook's lecture on Emerson and immortality. When Cook had spoken on the Trinity, Alcott, who had been hoping for what he called an ethical statement, was disappointed in hearing, rather, an expression that was merely dogmatic and rhetorical. But there were more agreeable relationships later, and presently Alcott was attending lectures with the Cooks and holding conversations at their home. Under such influences, and with the rising tide of orthodoxy in Boston, Alcott's religious views received added if not new coloring. At first, he admitted to himself that he entertained views, if not identical with evangelical orthodoxy, at least more in harmony with it, than he had in the days of his *Conversations on the Gospels*. If he mistook not, he was freed now from his earlier Unitarian bias. Later, when he had heard Cook many times, and the minister had pressed him for some statement of his convictions, Alcott was willing to say that, whatever beliefs he had entertained in the past, he now gladly accepted the Christian Trinity in its orthodox significances.

Nor was this all. When Cook had lectured on Emerson and immortality, he had questioned Alcott after the lecture about Emerson's views. Had he failed to comprehend them? Emerson was so loyal to his instincts, Alcott answered, that he would not name his creed: pantheistic, theistic, or even Christian. Intellectually his creed might be tinged with pantheism, but at heart Emerson was theistic and Christian.[26] Then, after the relations with Cook had matured, and Alcott had often spoken in evangelical pulpits, Emerson published his "Sovereignty of Ethics" in the *North American Review*. Alcott had attended a meeting of the Fortnightly Club at Sanborn's one evening early in May, and had heard the newly published essay read to the club. It was agreed at this meeting, he wrote in his diary afterward, that in this essay Emerson had more fully written out his views than in former essays, and that he now took his place with the Christian theists and great moral teachers of the past. Thereafter, in his conversations at Cook's and elsewhere, Alcott permitted the newspapers to report him as saying that Emerson had changed his basic views. In his diary he wrote that, whatever the claim of other religious groups, Cook plainly had the right to class Emerson with the orthodox theists.[27]

It was, of course, sad—this little tempest in a small teapot. The paragraphs which made up "The Sovereignty of Ethics" had been drawn from several old lectures—some of them sixteen or nineteen years old—and put together by James Elliot Cabot, who had been helping Emerson arrange the text for his last book.[28] They represented no new thought, but only seemed to do so in the excitement of Cook's eagerness and in the reactions of the day. As for Alcott, he had never, in his maturity, spoken of himself as a pantheist; hence his belief in his old age that he was freeing himself from such views was a false transposition of terms.

His friend Cook had been a poor intellectual guide. If Alcott had reflected, he would of course have remembered that Emerson could not have made pantheism a logical outcome of Fichte's teachings, as Cook said, because Emerson knew little about Fichte and cared nothing about what he knew. His thoughts had had quite another origin, as had Alcott's too, and they were not pantheistic. But Alcott, like Emerson, was now an old man, and it was difficult for him to remember things out of the distant past.

Happily these misunderstandings were speedily terminated. When Cook's assertions about Emerson's renunciations of belief had become widespread, Emerson gave his son permission to say that his views were to be found in his essays, and not elsewhere.[29]

In his diary Alcott carefully pasted the clipping containing Emerson's denial. As for himself, it seemed agreed that he was sufficiently orthodox to be claimed no longer by Unitarians, either of the conservative or of the radical type, but Emerson's faith appeared to remain a debatable question still. Well, it would be a difficult matter for any sect to classify either of them.[30]

v

When Alcott was in his eighty-second year, he made his farthermost lecture and conversation tour. His tall, spare figure was dressed in clerical black. He wore a high collar and a black satin stock, and his long white hair hung down to his shoulders. His whole appearance suggested the mode of a past generation.

Out in the capital of the young state of Iowa, people were still curious about Emerson's religious views. Alcott's answer was simple.

Emerson, said he, was an essayist, and not a theologian.[31]

WINTER GLACIERS

THOUGH HE WAS NOW an octogenarian, Alcott experienced no cessation of interest in life—felt, rather, an upsurge of enthusiasm, and a great pleasure in the late prosperity of his ambitions. If there was sadness mingled with this happiness, that, perhaps, was only what an old man might expect.

As in the days when he had first moved to Concord, and had found the air and sun so genial while he worked in his garden at the Hosmer cottage, the simple aspects of nature renewed his old idyllic sentiments. He was happy to walk in his garden when his strawberries were in their prime, and noted with satisfaction how superior and profuse they were. The strawberry, he thought, was the queen of berries. Though he no longer walked to Walden now, he still drove there with Sanborn, and found swimming in the cove near Henry's hermitage as inviting as ever. In February, when the first fair days melted the snow, and warm tints appeared in the landscape, he imagined that he could already scent the spring in the air. Then came the spring breezes, and the bluebird's song. In such bland airs, and with such abundant foliage brightening each successive day, it was a luxury to be alive. The view from his hilltop, over Mill Brook, and toward Lincoln Wood, was as charming as ever. On May mornings, when the apple blossoms were in their full beauty and fragrance, it was as if he were sipping youth again, or having his first draught of immortality. Rapture, it seemed to him, best expressed the emotion thus kindled into sweet satisfactions. What were the theologian's cunning arguments compared to the odors and shows of spring for proofs of the Divinity shining through the eternal seasons' rounds? What name so real, what presence so near, as His who spread abroad this splendid spectacle? It seemed to Alcott, on such days as these, that all things preached a present Deity.

In these last years, however, there had been sorrows, too. The heart troubles and dropsy which had attacked Mrs. Alcott left her feeble and sad, never again to be the family's brave and energetic leader. Two weeks after she and her husband and Louisa had moved to join Anna, who was a widow and lived in the Thoreau house on Main Street, Mrs. Alcott was dead. His days must be very different now, Alcott saw, than when she was at his side to prompt to instant duty, though her life, so full of sacrifices, would be a sweet and gentle memory. Then, only two years later, came the news of May's death. May had been in Europe studying art. She had been praised by Ruskin for her copies of Turner, and had had a still life accepted at the Paris salon. She had been married happily a year when her baby was born, though thereafter she had lived less than two months. Emerson had come carrying the telegram announcing the sad news. He had been pale and tearful, and unable to speak—he, their best and tenderest friend. But May's bright career had been closed, Alcott assured himself, only to open for her a wider stage and holier joys in another existence. Such thoughts, too, had been his solace as Mrs. Alcott lay ill and half-conscious all day, whispering to herself the unspeakable raptures she enjoyed as a foretaste of the bliss she was soon to partake in its fullness.[1]

But if there had been sorrows for Alcott, there were honors likewise to persuade him that he had not waited in vain during the long years when his lips were sealed save to a few friends and to small companies. His long apprenticeship in the school of leisure was drawing to a close and bringing something like a late ripeness of gifts for usefulness in his time. When Harvard had made him an honorary member of Phi Beta Kappa,[2] he was pleased with the dignity thus added to his name, and recalled how, in the early days of their acquaintance, when the doors of the élite had still been closed to him, Emerson had brought him to the exercises of the society, assuring him that he was a member by right of genius. Now he attended meetings as a fellow member, and saw with pleasure, at the dinners, the long rows of guests rise at the tables when Emerson's name was mentioned by the president. At the West his lectures and conversations were no longer a novelty, and he might have almost whatever parlors, pulpits, or platforms he cared to choose. Now, even in New England he was being asked to speak. But his greatest happiness lay in the success of the Concord School of Philosophy, the realization of the hopes for an ideal university which he had first discussed with Emerson forty years ago, and something of the kind that Sanborn, too, had planned when he had first come to Concord. When, at last, the chapel was built on the grounds of Orchard House, nothing could have pleased him more. His associations with the place were, he thought, of the happiest and holiest kind. Twenty years of toil had shaped and hallowed it; now, dedicated to these high uses and ends, his labors were consummated as he could have wished.[3]

He still saw Emerson, though their walks together, except, sometimes, to the post office and back, had ceased many years ago. Emerson came now and then to spend an evening, but such a visit Alcott now considered a rare favor. Much more often it was he who called at Emerson's—sometimes in the evening when company gathered to hear a paper read or when he himself conducted a conversation, but more often to dine alone with Emerson, or to take tea

with him in the afternoon. On the latter occasions, they
renewed their old subjects. Shakespeare remained for
Emerson the one scholar whom the world had yet produced,
and another like him could only come in the far future.[4]
Emerson told again the story of his meeting with Wordsworth at Rydal Mount—how the old Wordsworth, standing apart in the garden walk, had recited his latest sonnets,
like a schoolboy declaiming! Once the friends read together
a letter from Alexander Ireland, who had arranged Emerson's English lecture tour, a letter in which it was said that
Carlyle's health was still vigorous, and that his powers of
conversation were unimpaired—though he was now in his
eighties! Emerson was rereading Margaret Fuller's letters
and was finding them, after these thirty years or more, even
more brilliant and remarkable than he had supposed. Occasionally, too, the friends still spoke of their old interest
in Thomas Taylor and his translations, which they had
separately discovered before they had known each other in
their early manhood; or, most rarely of all, Emerson
brought out his diaries and they would spend the hours in
pleasant reminiscence.[5] Alcott was no longer reluctant as
formerly to visit Emerson for fear of breaking in upon his
work, for Emerson assured him that he had ceased to write
—scarcely wrote even a letter—no longer wished to lecture,
and preferred best of all to sit in his study and read.

And yet, though a rich leisure now invited a closer
fellowship, Alcott was saddened by the realization that they
were being held apart and, indeed, separated farther and
farther, by forces which neither could control. It was, of
course, a gradual process. Emerson was complaining of
growing old, that his memory was failing, that he could no
longer find the words he wished to speak. And so he was
withdrawing deeper and deeper into solitude. It was
pathetic, Alcott thought, to sit in Emerson's parlor when

company gathered there, to hear his friend's expressive silences, to see him smilingly present, and with sympathetic glances, yet saying scarcely a word.[6] When Emerson read a lecture, as he still occasionally did, with Ellen present to turn his pages for him and to suggest what paragraphs to omit, it was no longer the brilliant and impressive spectacle that it once had been, when he was the inspired rhapsodist uttering oracles with a charm rare and unsurpassed. To those who had seen him then, these latter performances were by no means attractive, nor their repetition desirable. Presently, too, even private conversation with him became more and more difficult. If Emerson's memory was failing him, Alcott had to confess that his own growing deafness rendered conversation less satisfactory than formerly, especially since Emerson latterly was falling progressively into subdued and inaudible undertones. Besides, it was hardly profitable, it seemed to Alcott, to tell his friend of his latest adventures with lectures and conversations, since these would pass from his memory with the telling.[7] There was no denying that the former brightness of their intimacy had been lessened and obscured. Age was doing its work upon his friend, Alcott perceived, and he felt not a little anxious concerning his stay; nor did he wish the shadow when the substance was so far withdrawn from view. It was an unexpected close of so fair a display of gifts.

There was, however, one last pleasant meeting in Emersons' study, on a Thursday in mid-April, when Alcott came to bring a copy of his latest book, his *Sonnets and Canzonets*. Emerson read several of the sonnets aloud with emphasis and apparent delight, and Alcott was proud that his friend should enjoy these last works of his pen.[8]

II

A few days later, on the cloudless morning of April 26, Alcott walked to Emerson's and was admitted to the upstairs chamber where Emerson lay ill with pneumonia.[9] Ellen announced the visitor, and as Emerson turned in his bed to greet his friend, it was, it seemed to Alcott, with a glance and smile such as none other could give. There was an affectionate clasp of the hand, and words of farewell in a voice that faltered and fell into indistinctness.

Above him, as Alcott walked homeward, the morning sun shone brightly. Yes, but the light that had illuminated his friendship so long and sweetly was overcast, and he knew that he was soon to be left alone.

NOTES

ACKNOWLEDGMENTS

The chief sources for this study have been the ten volumes of Ralph Waldo Emerson's *Journals* (Boston: The Riverside Press, 1909-1914), and the fifty manuscript Journals of Amos Bronson Alcott. I have also referred with less frequency to the typed copies of the manuscript Journals of Emerson housed in Widener Library, Harvard University.

Other sources include: Amos Bronson Alcott's *Concord Days* (Boston: Roberts Brothers, 1888); James E. Cabot's *A Memoir of Ralph Waldo Emerson* (2 vols., Boston: Houghton Mifflin and Company, 1887); Ednah D. Cheney's *Louisa May Alcott; Her Life, Letters, and Journals* (Boston: Roberts Brothers, 1890); George Willis Cooke's *An Historical and Biographical Introduction to Accompany the Dial* (2 vols., Cleveland: The Rowfant Club, 1902); the *Dial;* Ralph Waldo Emerson's *Complete Works* (12 vols., Boston: Houghton Mifflin and Company, 1904); Edward Waldo Emerson's *Emerson in Concord* (Boston: Houghton Mifflin and Company, 1890); Charles Eliot Norton's *The Correspondence of Thomas Carlyle and Ralph Waldo Emerson* (Boston: Houghton Mifflin and Company, 1894); Ralph L. Rusk's *The Letters of Ralph Waldo Emerson* (6 vols., New York: Columbia University Press, 1939); F. B. Sanborn's *The Personality of Emerson* (Boston: Goodspeed, 1903); F. B. Sanborn's and W. T. Harris's *A. Bronson Alcott: His Life and Philosophy* (2 vols., Boston: Roberts Brothers, 1893); Clara Endicott Sears's *Bronson Alcott's Fruitlands* (Boston: Houghton Mifflin and Company, 1924); Henry David Thoreau's *Writings* (20 vols., Boston: Houghton Mifflin and Company, 1906).

I am indebted to Professor Edward W. Forbes of Cambridge, Massachusetts, for permission to consult the Emerson manuscripts in the Widener Library and to Mr. Frederic Wolsey Pratt of Concord, Massachusetts, for permission to read the Alcott manuscript Journals in the Concord Public Library.

Although I made no use of his excellent *Pedlar's Progress* or *The Journals of Bronson Alcott,* I am thankful to Professor Odell Shepard for great personal kindnesses. Miss Sarah Bartlett, librarian of the Concord Public Library, has been consistently helpful and gracious, and to her I wish to express my deepest gratitude.

To the Graduate College of the State University of Iowa, through Dean George D. Stoddard and Dean Carl E. Seashore, I am obligated for financial assistance in the pursuit of this study.

THIS THROBBING HEART

1. Alcott was a wide and an enthusiastic reader. A list of his readings, together with his reflections thereon, must be of importance to every literary historian of the nineteenth century. With what aims he read can be ascertained

from a number of his journal entries. On May 29, 1827, he makes "An outline of reading . . . to be read, in connection with writing and reflection during the ensuing season. . . . They shall not palm their opinions passively upon us; we will have the privilege to investigate for ourselves. We will depend upon our own powers. Reason shall be our guide in the pursuit of Truth." In July of the same year he proposes to keep "an Account of Books read, serving for an Index to the Mind; shaping its character; and presenting a history of mental development." References, unless otherwise indicated, are to Alcott's MS Journals housed in the Concord Public Library, Concord, Massachusetts, and belonging to Mr. Frederic Wolsey Pratt.

2. Locke, Stewart, and Reid are mentioned for the first time on May 29, 1827. (The Journals begin in 1826.) On July 9, 1829, Alcott ardently favors Locke. On March 15, 1831, Pascal seems equally interesting. Some time before March, 1829, Alcott had read Reid's *Observations on the Growth of the Mind.*

3. Alcott's intermittent remarks on Dr. Channing and other Boston divines begin on April 27, 1828.

4. See especially the Journal entries for October, 1832, and February, 1833.

5. The Thomas Taylor volume of Plato came into Alcott's hands in May, 1833.

6. Journal, September 28, 1828.

7. Alcott quoted in F. B. Sanborn and W. T. Harris, *A. Bronson Alcott: His Life and Philosophy* (Boston, 1893), I, 44.

8. Benjamin K. Emerson and George A. Gordon, *The Ipswich Emersons, 1836-1900* (Boston, 1900).

9. James Elliot Cabot, *A Memoir of Ralph Waldo Emerson* (Boston, 1887), pp. 78-97, *passim.*

10. Ralph Waldo Emerson, *Journals* (Cambridge, Mass., 1909-1914), II, 180. Since most of Emerson's diary has been published, it is to the published volumes that reference will herein be made—unless otherwise indicated.

11. *Ibid.,* II, 330-345. De Gerando was important in shaping Emerson's thought, not only as related to the Greeks, but to the Orientals as well.

12. *Ibid.,* II, 348-350.

13. *Ibid.,* II, 495-500.

14. Emerson remarks on his European friends in his *Journals,* III, 3-220, and in his *English Traits (The Complete Works of Ralph Waldo Emerson,* Concord Edition, Cambridge, Mass., 1904), pp. 3-24. The last of these *Journal* passages show how his reflections were crystallizing for the writing of *Nature.*

A SEEING EYE

1. Emerson, *Journals,* III, 501, 509, 511, 559.

2. Sanborn and Harris, *op. cit.,* I, 240-241; Alcott's MS Journals, June 2, 1875.

3. Alcott, *op. cit.,* February 3, 1836.

4. *Ibid.,* September 11, 1836.

5. *Ibid.,* May, 1837.

6. Emerson, *op. cit.,* IV, 235-240, *passim.*

7. Alcott, *op. cit.,* June, 1838.

8. Emerson, *op. cit.,* IV, 450, 459, 469.

9. *Ibid.*, V, 308; Alcott, *op. cit.*, November 1, 1839.

10. Emerson, *op. cit.*, V, 174-175.

11. Alcott, *op. cit.*, November 23 and December 19, 1839.

12. Emerson, *op. cit.*, V, 219, 322.

THE QUEST OF THE ABSOLUTE

1. Ralph L. Rusk (ed.), *The Letters of Ralph Waldo Emerson* (New York, 1939), II, 313.

2. His MS Journal from 1839 to 1846 is no longer extant. The reflections are from the *Dial*, II, 409-437 (April, 1842).

3. Emerson's MS Journals, "Notebook A. B. A.," 1937 (typewritten) copy, Widener Library, Cambridge, Massachusetts.

4. Emerson, *Journals*, VI, 169-178.

5. *Ibid.*, VI, 46-47.

6. *Ibid.*, VI, 258-264; Nathaniel Hawthorne, *The American Note-Books* (*The Complete Writings of Nathaniel Hawthorne*, Old Manse Edition, Boston, 1900), pp. 412-413.

7. Charles Lane, "A. Bronson Alcott's Works," *Dial*, III, 418-454 (April, 1843).

8. Emerson, *op. cit.*, VI, 291.

9. *Ibid.*, VI, 392-393, 396; V, 473-474; *Essays, Second Series*, pp. 101 and 312 n.

10. The best source for factual information regarding Fruitlands remains Clara Endicott Sears's *Bronson Alcott's Fruitlands* (Boston, 1915), the chief source here used.

11. Emerson, *op. cit.*, VI, 420-421. Emerson's diary for this period has many references to the Fruitlanders, as have his letters.

12. See Sears, *Bronson Alcott's Fruitlands*, and G. W. Cooke, *An Historical and Biographical Introduction to Accompany the Dial* (Cleveland, 1902), II, 154-159.

13. Rusk, *op. cit.*, III, 230.

14. Sears, *Bronson Alcott's Fruitlands*, p. 111.

15. Emerson, *op. cit.*, VI, 503-505.

DEAR AND COMELY FORMS

1. The skeptical elements in Emerson's thought are best illustrated in "Experience," "Montaigne," "Fate," and "Illusions." See also *Journals*, VII, 289-290.

2. Emerson, *Journals*, VII, 303.

3. *Ibid.*, VII, 60-61, 321.

4. *Ibid.*, VII, 253, 305-306.

5. Clara Endicott Sears (ed.), *Gleanings from Old Shaker Journals* (Boston, 1916), p. 268.

6. Alcott's MS Journals, January 1, 1847.

7. *Ibid*, March 16, 1847.

8. *Ibid.*, June 28, 1846.

9. Ednah D. Cheney (ed.), *Louisa May Alcott: Her Life, Letters, and Journals* (Boston, 1890), p. 57.

10. Henry David Thoreau, *Familiar Letters* (*The Writings of Henry David Thoreau*, Boston, 1906), p. 151.

11. Emerson, *op. cit.*, VII, 446.

12. *Ibid.*, VII, 450-473, *passim;* Rusk, *op. cit.*, IV, 72-78.

13. Emerson, *op. cit.*, VII, 477-478.

14. *Ibid.*, VII, 344-459, *passim; English Traits*, pp. 273-280; Rusk, *op. cit.*, IV, 31-101, *passim.*

15. Emerson, *Journals*, VII, 524.

16. Thoreau, *Walden*, p. 294.

THE LONG LEVEL YEARS

1. Cheney, *op. cit.*, pp. 61-92, *passim.*

2. Emerson, *op. cit.*, VIII, 362-363, 519.

3. Rusk, *op. cit.*, IV, 514.

4. Cheney, *op. cit.*, pp. 69-70.

5. Emerson, *op. cit.*, VIII, 38-39, 562-563.

6. Alcott, *op. cit.*, August 15, 1856.

7. *Ibid.*, October 4, 1856.

8. A. Bronson Alcott, *Concord Days* (Boston, 1888), pp. 37-38.

9. *Columbian and Great West*, Cincinnati, June 1, 1850; St. Louis *Daily Evening News*, December 30, 1852; *Wisconsin State Journal*, Madison, February 7, 1860.

10. Emerson, "The American Scholar," *Nature, Addresses and Lectures*, pp. 94-95.

11. Emerson, *Journals*, VIII, 445; IX, 263; Rusk, *op. cit.*, V, 60.

12. Rusk, *op. cit.*, IV, 209-214.

13. Emerson, *op. cit.*, VIII, 231-234, 433, 473, 584-585.

14. Boston *Bee* quoted in Wm. Lloyd Garrison's *Liberator*, Boston, April 14, 1854; Cincinnati *Daily Enquirer*, February 1, 1860; Cabot, *op. cit.*, pp. 574-611; Alcott MS Journals, January, 1861.

15. Emerson, *op. cit.*, X, 473-474.

16. Alcott, *op. cit.*, September 7 and November 5, 1857.

17. Cheney, *op. cit.*, pp. 96-98; Alcott, *op. cit.*, February 5, 1858.

18. Alcott, *op. cit.*, January 4, 1859.

19. Cheney, *op. cit.*, pp. 126-127.

20. *Ibid.*, pp. 121-122, 149, 153-154.

21. Emerson, *op. cit.*, IX, 134, 221.

22. *Ibid.*, IX, 183, 273, 322, 536, 560-561.

23. *Ibid.*, IX, 44-45, 97, 113, 144, 425.

24. *Ibid.*, IX, 54, 180.

25. *Ibid.*, IX, 35-36.

26. *Ibid.*, IX, 59, 132.

27. Alcott, *op. cit.*, December 25, 1860, and February 16, 1861.

28. Emerson, *op. cit.*, IX, 503.

29. Alcott, *op. cit.*, May 23, 1864; July 19, 1871; MS Letters (typewritten copy) of William Ellery Channing to Ralph Waldo Emerson (in my possession), February 1, 1852, and November 20, 1868.

30. Alcott, *op. cit.*, January 1 and May 7, 1862; Emerson, *Journals*, IX, 425.

31. Emerson, *op. cit.*, X, 39-41.

FANCY DEPARTS

1. Emerson, *Poems*, pp. 489-490 n.
2. Rusk, *op. cit.*, V, 451, 455, 492.
3. Cabot, *op. cit.*, pp. 633-644.
4. Rusk, *op. cit.*, VI, 149-161; James B. Thayer, *A Western Journey with Mr. Emerson* (Boston, 1884); *Daily Alta California*, San Francisco, April 24, 1871.
5. Alcott, *op. cit.*, July 24 and 28, 1872.
6. Emerson, *Journals*, X, 396, 405; Rusk, *op. cit.*, VI, 226-227.
7. *Ibid.*, VI, 230, 233.
8. The visit to Virginia I have treated at some length in "Emerson in Virginia," *New England Quarterly*, V, 753-768 (October, 1932).
9. A. Bronson Alcott, *Ralph Waldo Emerson, Philosopher and Seer* (London, 1889), pp. v-vi, quoting Emerson's letter to Mrs. Stearns, July 5, 1865.
10. Alcott MS Journals, June 1, 1873, and December 27, 1876.
11. Cheney, *op. cit.*, pp. 190-266, *passim*.
12. Alcott, *op. cit.*, March 5, 1871.
13. *Ibid.*, March 29, 1869, and July 19, 1870.
14. *Ibid.*, November 10, 1868, and April 30, 1875.
15. Emerson, "The World-Soul," *Poems*, p. 19.
16. Emerson, *Journals*, X, 157-158.
17. *Ibid.*, X, 144.
18. *Ibid.*, X, 167, 287, 423, 463. The references to science are numerous in this volume.
19. *Ibid.*, X, 318, 321, 337.
20. *Ibid.*, X, 234, 277-278, 473.
21. *Ibid.*, X, 279.
22. *Ibid.*, X, 297.
23. *Ibid.*, X, 386.
24. Alcott, *op. cit.*, February 8, 1865.
25. *Ibid.*, May 29, 1870.
26. *Ibid.*, December 18, 1876, and December 15, 1879.
27. *Ibid.*, May 4 and December 1, 1878; August 23, 1879; January 12, 1880.
28. Emerson, *Lectures and Biographical Sketches*, p. 549 n.
29. Emerson, *Letters and Social Aims*, p. 416 n. Dr. Edward Waldo Emerson's statement appears in a letter dated February 17, 1880. A résumé appeared in the Concord *Freeman*, Concord, Massachusetts, March 4, 1880. The complete letter was published in George Willis Cooke's *Ralph Waldo Emerson: His Life, Writings, and Philosophy* (Boston, 1882), pp. 363-364 n., and in the Indianapolis *Journal*, April 28, 1882. In both sources it is represented as "written . . . to a gentleman in Indianapolis."
30. Alcott, *op. cit.*, February 16, 1880.
31. *Ibid.*, March 26, 1881. I have told somewhat of Alcott's Western experiences in "Some Iowa Lectures and Conversations of Amos Bronson Alcott," *Iowa Journal of History and Politics*, XXIX, 375-401 (July, 1931).

WINTER GLACIERS

1. Alcott, *op. cit.*, November 25, 1877, and December 31, 1879.
2. *Ibid.*, November 18, 1874.
3. *Ibid.*, April 28, 1880.
4. *Ibid.*, March 8, 1878.
5. *Ibid.*, March 26, 1879.
6. *Ibid.*, January 25 and March 8, 1882.
7. *Ibid.*, May 21, 1881.
8. *Ibid.*, April 13, 1882.
9. *Ibid.*, April 26, 1882.

INDEX